Praise for *Mo*

"Adam Taylor has written a beautiful, inspiring book. The message is pure and true: faith transforms people, and transformed people can transform the world. For me, reading the book was itself a transformative experience, a necessary reminder of how my own faith inspires and commands me to change injustice into justice, callousness into compassion, conflict into cooperation."

EBOO PATEL, founder and executive director, Interfaith Youth Core

"In *Mobilizing Hope* Adam Taylor challenges Christians to embrace St. Paul's call not to conform with the ways of the world but to be people of conviction and action and hope. The book offers practical examples and ideas for putting our faith to work on behalf of the poor and oppressed."

RICHARD STEARNS, president, World Vision, U.S., and author of *The Hole in Our Gospel*

"This theologically reflective and historically thoughtful book is the result of an embodied life of justice. *Mobilizing Hope* reveals the very best of what the next evangelicalism can be. Passionate about Jesus with a deep sense of God's heart of justice for the world, Adam's work challenges all of us to live an authentic spirituality and a lived theology for the sake of the gospel and the world."

SOONG-CHAN RAH, Milton B. Engebretson Associate Professor of Church Growth and Evangelism, North Park Theological Seminary

"Adam Taylor is a true prophet of our time. From the halls of Harvard to the West Wing of the White House to the streets of Zimbabwe, he has been a consistent voice for justice and righteousness. His message echoes the Old Testament prophets who were unafraid to speak truth to power. But Taylor's secret is he knows movements don't start in the halls of power; they end there. In *Mobilizing Hope,* Taylor shares how our generation can birth a new Spirit-led movement for justice."

AARON GRAHAM, lead pastor, The District Church

"I highly recommend *Mobilizing Hope* to men and women who are crazy enough to believe that our faith should lead to action, and that our action offers hope for a transformed society. Adam is a dynamic young leader with much wisdom to offer those of us engaged in the complexities of seeking justice."

NOEL CASTELLANOS, CEO, Christian Community Development Association

"Adam Taylor's daring manifesto calls a new generation of faith leaders to become Christ-centered activists for love and justice. Inspired by Martin Luther King Jr.'s dream, Taylor's *Mobilizing Hope* offers a bold, vivid vision that energizes and equips Christians to live into a prophetic, intercultural future."

PETER GOODWIN HELTZEL, author of *Jesus and Justice*

"Adam Taylor makes a powerful case for a new chapter of activism for the common good, and he provides practical guidance for those who heed the call. Taylor treasures his heritage; he also understands the hopes and fears of a new generation about civic engagement. By candidly and perceptively addressing these matters, Taylor creates a new conversation and points toward a better day."

MELISSA ROGERS, director of the Center for Religion and Public Affairs, Wake Forest University Divinity School

"Adam Taylor's *Mobilizing Hope* will likely be one of the prompts that we've long needed to calibrate our moral compasses and the spark we've needed to refocus our attention on reconciliation and justice in the post-civil rights era. This book speaks to the new generation of leaders, as well as the vanguard, about what it takes to transition from service to activism and what each of us needs to do to find a voice that is clear and truthful in the twenty-first century."

ROBERT FRANKLIN, president, Morehouse College

"In *Mobilizing Hope,* Adam Taylor issues a most compassionate, compelling and courageous call for a new generation of transformed kingdom-focused nonconformists and activists committed to social and economic justice as the saving grace of America. He draws upon his own homegrown roots as a student of the 1960s Civil Rights Movement's messages and methods. Yet, he recognizes that today's young leaders will frame strategies that fit new times. His bottom line, and that of God's people of diverse backgrounds, must be to ignore society's seductive call to conform and answer the gospel call to dismantle injustice wherever it is found."

DR. BARBARA WILLIAMS-SKINNER, president, Skinner Leadership Institute, former executive director, Congressional Black Caucus

"Adam Taylor challenges and upends the pervasive notion that narcissism and cynicism define his contemporaries, and provides a comprehensive field guide for their burgeoning hope."

PAUL FARMER, M.D., Ph.D., Presley Professor, Harvard Medical School

ADAM TAYLOR
FOREWORD BY JIM WALLIS

MOBILIZING HOPE

FAITH-INSPIRED ACTIVISM FOR A POST–CIVIL RIGHTS GENERATION

MARTA,

I pray this book
Inspires you to mobilize
hope for generations to
come. Adam T

IVP Books

An imprint of InterVarsity Press
Downers Grove, Illinois

InterVarsity Press
P.O. Box 1400, Downers Grove, IL 60515-1426
World Wide Web: www.ivpress.com
E-mail: email@ivpress.com

InterVarsity Press® is the book-publishing division of InterVarsity Christian Fellowship/USA®,
a movement of students and faculty active on campus at hundreds of universities, colleges and
schools of nursing in the United States of America, and a member movement of the International
Fellowship of Evangelical Students. For information about local and regional activities, write
Public Relations Dept., InterVarsity Christian Fellowship/USA, 6400 Schroeder Rd., P.O. Box
7895, Madison, WI 53707-7895, or visit the IVCF website at <www.intervarsity.org>.

All Scripture quotations, unless otherwise indicated, are taken from the Holy Bible, New
International Version®. NIV®. Copyright ©1973, 1978, 1984 by International Bible Society.
Used by permission of Zondervan Publishing House. All rights reserved.

Design: Cindy Kiple
Images: alohaspirit/iStockphoto

ISBN 978-0-8308-3837-0

Printed in the United States of America ∞

Library of Congress Cataloging-in-Publication Data

Taylor, Adam, 1976-
    Mobilizing hope: faith-inspired activism for a post-civil rights
generation/Adam Taylor.
        p. cm.
    Includes bibliographical references (p.).
    ISBN 978-0-8308-3837-0 (pbk.: alk. paper)
 1. Youth in church work. 2. Social justice—Religious
aspects—Christianity.   3. Radicalism—Religious
aspects—Christianity.   I. Title.
    BV4427.T39 2010
    253.084'2—dc22
                                                                    2010019857

P	18	17	16	15	14	13	12	11	10	9	8	7	6	5	4	3	2	1
Y	25	24	23	22	21	20	19	18	17	16	15	14	13	12	11	10

CONTENTS

THE NEXT GENERATION

ADAM TAYLOR, more than any young leader I have met, exemplifies the best of the next generation of Christian activists. He was first a student of mine at Harvard's Kennedy School; then my course assistant; then I joined the board of Global Justice, the student network that Adam started; then he joined our board at Sojourners; then he became my senior political director; then he became a White House Fellow. Adam has become my friend, kindred spirit and younger soulmate in the movement to put faith into action.

Mobilizing Hope is his first book, and is a manifesto for this generation, which is such a sign of hope for me. This important book is five things at the same time.

First, it is a *story*—partly Adam's story and partly the story of his many cohorts who are shaping the next strategies for faith-based social change. Adam understands the power of story, and this book invites readers to connect their own story to the history of social justice. Adam integrates his life experience with a new generation's guide to organizing. He describes his beginning activism in high school and through college, his trips to South Africa, and his continuing education in contemporary social movements. He draws on those experiences to analyze campaigns, strategy and tactics learned from his work with Global AIDS, the Jubilee debt relief movement and Sojourners.

Second, it is a *theology* for social justice, full of biblical references, reflections and metaphors that point to God's intentions and future for the world. This is not an argument rooted in political ideology but a vision for social justice rooted firmly in the Scriptures. It does not conform to the old categories of left and right but seeks to hold both sides accountable to a biblical ethic which isn't politically predictable. It sheds old baggage and polarities, and speaks to a new generation looking for new options. In doing so, *Mobilizing Hope* opens up the possibilities of new alliances and constituencies for both moral and political transformation.

Third, it is a *spirituality* for young activists, with the mature understanding that if you want to be a person of justice and action, and last for very long, you must also become a person of prayer and contemplation. I know how real and important *faith* is to Adam, and it motivates every page of this book. Most important, he believes that the foundation of any social movement is people whose faith leads them to believe that change is possible. He knows that hope always precedes change. Hope is the substance of faith, and the only absolutely indispensable ingredient for individual and social transformation. When we look at history, there is a spiritual chain of events: faith that leads to hope, hope that produces action, and action that leads to change. It is that sequence that has empowered all successful social movements, and it is one that Adam Taylor understands.

Fourth, *Mobilizing Hope* is a *handbook* for those who want to experiment with activism and search out their own vocation in changing the world. It is a guidebook for *how* to make a difference, with many examples of what works and what does not. As I speak around the country, I meet a growing number of young Christians who want to put their faith into action for social justice. They've done mission trips to urban America and around the world, and seen the hunger, poverty and disease that afflicts so many of God's children. They want to change that reality, to move beyond just service, but they don't know where or how to begin. *Mobilizing Hope* offers a starting point.

Fifth, it is a *strategy* manual. Adam consciously draws on lessons from past movements for change, particularly the civil rights movement (this is a good introductory primer for some of those events and movements). He recognizes that we cannot simply duplicate past movements, but unless we learn from them, we are in danger of losing the connection between generations. And he strikes the right balance between building on the legacy of past movements while creatively trying new strategies and tactics. Adam shows how to draw from historical movements to develop new forms of organizing and advocacy that can meet our current realities.

Adam quotes one of my favorite lines from Dr. Martin Luther King Jr., "This hour in history needs a dedicated circle of transformed nonconformists." That belief is the core of the book, the importance of a committed minority of transformed nonconformists who creatively apply their faith in fresh, bold and innovative ways. This book intends to inspire and mobilize a new generation to become part of that prophetic minority.

From now on, whenever I meet those eager and seeking young people who want their faith and their lives to make a difference in the world, I have a book to recommend. And I commend it to you. It could change your life.

Jim Wallis
Founder and president, Sojourners

INTRODUCTION
THE TRANSFORMED NONCONFORMIST

Ain't gonna let nobody turn me around, turn me around,
turn me around. . . . I'm gonna keep on walkin', keep on talkin',
marching up the freedom lane.

FREEDOM SINGERS

IN MY FAVORITE SERMON by Dr. Martin Luther King Jr., "The Transformed Nonconformist," the civil rights leader offers a penetrating diagnosis of the culture of his time along with an equally compelling prescription:

> This hour in history needs a dedicated circle of transformed nonconformists. Our planet teeters on the brink of atomic annihilation; dangerous passions of pride, hatred, and selfishness are enthroned in our lives; truth lies prostrate on the rugged hills of nameless cavalries; and men do reverence before false gods of nationalism and materialism. The saving of our world from pending doom will come, not

through the complacent adjustment of the conforming majority, but through the creative maladjustment of a nonconforming minority.[1]

Dr. King is preaching from the apostle Paul's epistle to the Romans in which he offers a forewarning about the ensnaring influence of societal patterns upon our lives. Instead of living out the countercultural patterns of Christ, we find ourselves conforming to the patterns of this world. Paul writes:

> Therefore, I urge you, brothers, in view of God's mercy, to offer your bodies as living sacrifices, holy and pleasing to God—this is your spiritual act of worship. Do not conform any longer to pattern of this world, but be transformed by the renewing of your mind. Then you will be able to test and approve what God's will is—his good, pleasing and perfect will. (Romans 12:1-2)

Patterns of this world often become so normalized that we barely question their validity and often fail to comprehend the degree to which they circumscribe so much of our existence, keeping us from living our lives with a kingdom-like purpose and meaning. Patterns die hard, particularly when they become camouflaged as tradition or concealed as an immutable status quo. Patterns of this world can deceive and distract us, clouding our sense of calling.

Patterns are modes of thinking and acting that often become ingrained in our lives. According to sociologists, patterns are learned behaviors that become internalized and socialized. Anthropologists contend that patterns are culturally mediated and acquired. Psychologists posit that patterns represent cognitive records that shape our behavior. Theologians argue that patterns are the consequence of free will and that life-negating patterns are the result of separation from God's will.

According to Paul, as long as we accommodate to the cultural norms and paradigms of the world, we will be unable to fully experience God's perfect will in our lives. The path of least resistance is to complacently adjust to what the conforming majority says and does. This is true both in and outside the church, as our religious institutions have too often become just as conformed to the patterns of this world as the rest of society. To paraphrase Dr. King, too often the church has become a thermometer that measures the temperature of society rather than a thermostat that works to change it. This is not to say that all civic and religious culture has gone astray and needs adjusting. But patterns that reinforce selfishness, greed, nativism and violence are antithetical to biblical values and should offend our moral compass.

While many patterns make us feel good, they often provide a false sense of security or freedom. When we see others doing the same thing we feel justified to continue with an attitude or action that we know is of the world and not of the Spirit. While some patterns are innocuous, others, particularly those that lead us to perpetuate or ignore injustice, are pernicious. In contrast, God's patterns are by design life giving and life affirming. Vigilance is required to distinguish between God's ordained patterns and the patterns of the world.

A younger generation is growing increasingly thirsty for new patterns that reflect a renewed commitment to social justice. They are responding to the ever-present gravitational pull toward justice that has moved their predecessors to action. These tremors of activism necessitate new fountains of action and reflection anchored in hope.

In the face of seemingly intractable and often overwhelming crises we must become what Archbishop Desmond Tutu calls "prisoners of hope." Hope provides the inspirational and motivational bridge from our presently broken reality to a preferred future. Mobilizing hope requires breaking out of and replacing some patterns that have limited the in-breaking of God's kingdom. Instead, we must internalize Paul's call to become creatively maladjusted.

ACTIVISM FOR A POST–CIVIL RIGHTS GENERATION

When Dr. King delivered this sermon in 1963, the arc of the civil rights movement was in full swing. The movement was forcing America to face up to the contradictions and evils of Jim Crow segregation. This movement epitomized creative maladjustment fueled by the transformative power of nonviolent social change. Through sit-ins at lunch counters, voter-registration drives, marches and grueling door-to-door education, people of all ages worked to dismantle an unjust and oppressive system of racial subordination and transform people's hearts and minds. Acting out of a deep-seated faith from which they drew moral courage, movement leaders possessed the moral imagination to see an alternative reality in spite of the odds. While it can be counterproductive to overly romanticize previous movements, subsequent generations are slowly losing touch with a sense of what social movements can accomplish and the innovations that are necessary to expose and combat injustice today.

In high school I became addicted to the history of the civil rights movement. To this day I still pop in one of my prized tapes of the award-winning series *Eyes on the Prize* in order to get an extra dose of inspiration. Yet to many young people today, the Student Nonviolent Coordinating Committee (SNCC), Congress of Racial Equality (CORE) and even the Southern Christian Leadership Congress (SCLC) represent obscure and antiquated acronyms. SNCC was a multiracial movement led and driven by young people that often pushed the envelope, dramatizing the brutality and inhumanity of segregation. It is as though the reverence and awe that I feel toward SNCC is fading among a younger generation, like music deemed "old school."

Every generation can take for granted the struggles that came before them. However, in my generation's case, there is more going on than simply amnesia or lack of concern. Part of what is making us feel disconnected from civic activism is the degree to which the challenges and injustices of our current age have morphed into much more covert and institutionalized forms. Injustice continues to adapt to its new environment.

Yet we can't be held hostage to history, simply memorializing activism from the past. Instead, we must reinvent activism in ways that meet the challenges of our present reality. Many of the challenges from the 1960s such as economic injustice and inequality persist, even if they are harder to detect. Meanwhile, new challenges such as global climate change, terrorism and the prison industrial complex have emerged that test our resolve to God's kingdom-building project.

Social and political activism needs a better public relations manager. Activism is all too often associated with derelicts, rabble-rousers, radicals and extremists. This is in part because activists often defy authority, go against the grain and spark controversy. But they also plant seeds of change in society and surface issues that would otherwise go ignored. Almost unconsciously we celebrate a long legacy of activism. America's founding fathers were activists against oppressive British rule. Gandhi was an activist against the imperial British occupation of India. Rosa Parks was an activist in refusing to give up her seat on numerous occasions in Montgomery, Alabama, before being arrested and kick-starting a bus boycott that ignited a movement. Harriet Tubman was an activist who guided slaves to their freedom through the Underground Railroad. Archbishop Desmond Tutu was an activist fighting to dismantle the system of apartheid. Many of our most admired American and global leaders were activists. Most importantly, Christ was an activist who turned upside down the patterns of his world, ushering in a new kingdom that often stands in direct opposition to our earthly kingdom.

No one wants to be on the wrong side of God's movement of justice in history. When we look back, we often falsely believe that certain reforms in politics and transformations in society were inevitable, such as the end of the slave trade, Jim Crow segregation or apartheid in South Africa; however, these systems of injustice fell because of the tireless will and relentless sacrifice of a cadre of transformed nonconformists. If we are asked by our children, "Were you a part of the campaigns during the turn of the millennium that halted the global AIDS crisis, ended extreme poverty around the world, dramatically reduced domestic poverty in the United States, reversed global climate change, halted modern day forms of slavery, etc.?" what will be your answer? This book seeks to make that answer an emphatic yes.

What I love about Paul's message is that he goes on to emphasize that there is a unique role for every person who is willing to allow their life to become a living sacrifice. Paul goes on to write, "For as in one body we have many members, and not all the members have the same function, so we, who are many, are one body in Christ, and individually we are members one of another. We have gifts that differ according to the grace given to us: prophecy, in proportion to faith; ministry, in ministering; the teacher, in teaching; the exhorter, in exhortation; the giver, in generosity; the leader, in diligence; the compassionate, in cheerfulness" (Romans 12:4-8 NRSV). Similarly, in activism, we play different roles according to our unique gifts. Not everyone needs to be a gifted orator, brilliant strategist, policy expert or effective organizer. But everyone has a critical role to play according to God's design and purpose. Finding our role in social and political activism represents an integral part of Christian discipleship.

You are called to be an activist in the context where your gifts and passions meet the greatest needs around you. But we must all overcome patterns that numb us to the burning hurts in the world and must be rescued from the conformity that the world foists upon us. You must harness and use the gifts God has given you and work in concert with others with complementary gifts. There's an activist buried inside each and every one of us that is waiting to break free, like a sleeping lion that simply needs to be awakened by the right experiences, relationships and commitments.

My passion and core belief in the power of activism comes in part from my reading of history as well as from my practical, lived experience within a range of contexts locally, nationally and internationally. My forays into activism have come with a great deal of defeats and disappointments. However, the fulfillment and gratification I've experienced from victories large and small have enabled me to avoid becoming cynical or disillusioned. I have seen the empowering impact that activism can have on people's lives, and I have seen transformation take place within my own life as a result. Whether through my involvement in the global HIV/AIDS movement, living wage campaigns or the Jubilee movement to cancel developing countries' debt, I've witnessed people from many different walks of life effect tremendous change.

Inspired by Paul's message, Dr. King's quote provides the foundational purpose for this book: to inspire and mobilize a committed minority of transformed nonconformists who creatively apply their faith in fresh, bold and innovative ways. I believe that this committed minority possesses the power to lift us out of the muck and mire of our current reality to a higher ground of thought and action, and in the process accelerate the in-breaking of God's kingdom. By resisting some patterns and instead living out God's patterns, we will experience a more fulfilling, purposeful and abundant life.

Throughout this book I will try to provide real life examples of young leaders who have engaged in projects of transformed nonconformism. My hope is that you will be inspired by these stories and commit to embrace a more activist faith, joining a growing movement of transformed nonconformists who are mobilizing hope in ways that transform their communities, cities and world. Yes, I know, altar calls don't usually come until the end of a book or a sermon, but I thought I would present the invitation right from the beginning. It's only a sign of deep respect.

This committed minority of transformed nonconformists doesn't come from just one political persuasion or partisan affiliation. We are racially and ethnically diverse and don't fit neatly into the often broken political labels of liberal or conservative. These inherited categories fail to capture the complexities of the issues we face and tie us down into overly restrictive ideological categories. While I speak and act from a Christian faith perspective, one can also champion and embody social justice without being motivated by faith or because of another faith tradition. As Jim Wallis aptly says, religion does not have a monopoly on morality. However, this book is written primarily for people whose faith fuels their activism and is anchored in my Christian perspective.

Finally, this book seeks to close the gap between a growing concern for justice and an inability to channel that concern into tangible and sustainable change. This requires a deeper understanding of the systemic and structural nature of injustice as well as new tools for advocacy and organizing that are tailored to fit our current political, social and cultural landscape.

POURING NEW WINE INTO NEW WINESKINS

Jesus forewarns in the Gospels of Matthew, Mark and Luke, "Neither is new wine put into old wineskins; otherwise, the skins burst, and the wine is spilled, and the skins are destroyed; but new wine is put into fresh wineskins, and so both are preserved" (Matthew 9:17 NRSV). Every succeeding generation is faced with new circumstances and challenges distinct from their parents. Yet we inherit certain wineskins of how to engage in social and political change. My generation inherited the fruits of growing up as the first post–civil rights generation, never having directly experienced the inhumanity of Jim Crow segregation. We have never known Africa as a patchwork of European colonies and have long commemorated World AIDS Day and Earth Day. We were born too late to grow weary of the 1960s but just in time to be exposed to 60s nostalgia. We inherited the protest politics of the 60s, including the methods and mentalities developed through opposition to the Vietnam War and the cultural war over abortion. We were born in this in-between state, caught in the crossfire of the unfinished business of the civil rights struggle and the cultural backlash of the conservative movement.

Jesus' timeless wine truism helps lead us out of this conundrum. As disciples, we must have enough sense to reconcile the wine and wineskins of the past, preserving the good and throwing out that which no longer works. Every generation wields the potential of becoming new wine to our nation and world. The idealism, passion and imagination that are so often associated with youth provide combustible ingredients to spur social and political change. At our best, young people serve as the moral interrogators and conscience of the nation and world. Numerous historical examples prove this point, from the role of young people at the forefront of the civil rights movement to the anti-apartheid struggle. However, there is nothing inevitable about young people stepping into this transformative role. Conventional wisdom and the media suggest that this opportunity already skipped over Generation X and Y. Yet there is still time for these generations to redefine and reclaim a more active faith that gets applied in ways that confront and transform even the most intractable injustices.

New wineskins are necessary because our world has changed—the terrain for civic activism is different today than forty years ago due to the advent of the Internet, the twenty-four-hour news cycle and an increasingly integrated and globalized world. Previous social movements, including the civil rights movement, fell short of fully uprooting and changing a series of patterns that remain firmly entrenched today. The patterns that still must be resisted and transformed include: (1) a rugged individualism that often resembles a sanctified form of narcissism and comes at the expense of the common good; (2) a blind faith in market forces that reinforces a Darwinian, survival-of-the-fittest mentality; (3) a naive postracialism that hails racial progress while ignoring the ongoing need for racial justice and reconciliation; (4) a narrow nationalism that can make an idol out of America, conflating patriotism with military superiority and domination; and (5) an embrace of service and charity at the expense of a commitment to systemic justice. Each of these patterns will be unpacked and expanded on in later chapters.

Young people today also face a series of suffocating economic pressures and acute financial anxiety. The catapulting costs of higher education have pushed many to choose career paths based more on earning potential and the need to repay loans than on what they love and feel called to do. A majority of college graduates find themselves trapped in a vicious cycle of debt, which constrains their career options and exacerbates a sense of economic insecurity. An epidemic of credit card debt also contributes to these financial pressures. For instance, in 2004, two-thirds of four-year students graduated with loan debt averaging $19,200. Three out of four college students have credit cards that in 2005 carried an average unpaid balance of $2,169.[2] Meanwhile, many young people face stagnating wages for the majority of the work force and the reality of caring for aging parents who have lost their pensions and lack sufficient savings for retirement. While these trends crowd out the space and time for activism, they are not insurmountable and elevate the need for new forms of activism that account for such constraints.

As I will explore in further detail in chapter ten, young people have often replaced civic activism with community service. Community service encompasses a range of either isolated or ongoing efforts to meet human needs, often through the provision of some kind of social service; such as tutoring, refurbishing a school or preparing meals for the homeless. While noble and necessary, by itself, service can serve as a Band-Aid and result in dependency. In contrast, civic activism seeks to change the systems, decisions and policies that so often cause or exacerbate these needs. But not every need can be fulfilled purely through civic activism and policy or structural change. This demarcation is not a perfect one. Along the continuum between service and civic activism lies a series of actions designed to empower and develop communities.

Fortunately, a trend of declining civic activism is slowly reversing with voting among young Americans on the rise since 2000. An estimated twenty-three million young Americans under the age of thirty voted in the 2008 presidential election, 3.4 million more voters as compared to 2004. The Center for Information and Research on Civic Learning and Engagement (CIRCLE) estimated that youth voter turnout rose to between 52 percent and 53 percent, an increase of four to five percentage points since 2004. Compared to 2000, the increase in youth turnout is at least 11 percentage points.[3] Voting is just one indicator.

Young people are also embracing God's overriding concern for the weak, the vulnerable and the oppressed. However, this rising wave of concern has only just begun to translate into greater political and social activism. The 2008 election represents only the tip of the iceberg. President Obama's watershed victory was secured in part by the overwhelming support of black and Latino young people and a sizable shift in support among young white evangelicals. However, the shift can't be measured purely by voting patterns. It involves a broad range of engagement from consumer activism to lifestyle changes to social media.

Seeds of transformed nonconformism have been planted and are already bearing signs of fruit. A 2006 CIRCLE study[4] found that young people are working in many ways to improve their communities and the nation by volunteering, voting, protesting and raising money for charity and political candidates. In 2005, more

than 36 percent of young people ages fifteen to twenty-five volunteered, nearly 20 percent were involved with solving community
problems, 30 percent boycotted a product because of the conditions under which it was made or the values of the company that
made it.

Yet most young Americans remain misinformed about important aspects of politics and current events. For example, 53 percent
were unaware that only citizens can vote in federal elections; only
30 percent could correctly name at least one member of the president's cabinet; and only 34 percent knew that the United States has
a permanent seat on the United Nations Security Council. Young
people are also increasingly losing faith in government. Two-thirds
of young people believed that government should do more to solve
problems, but a plurality said that the government is "almost always wasteful and inefficient." This represents a big drop in confidence since 2002.[5]

In my travels to college campuses, churches and conferences
across the country, I've encountered young Christians who are asking penetrating questions about their faith. This generation of young
adults came of age at the crossfire of red and blue America. They are
also the byproduct of the schism between the mainline church's embrace of the social gospel and the evangelical focus on personal faith
and evangelism. How these young Christians approach the intersection of faith and politics can either deepen these divisions or instead
offer a road map to reconcile and transcend them.

Fortunately, many young Christians are rediscovering the
countercultural and radical demands of following Christ, cir-
cumventing the televangelists and prognosticators, and going
directly to the Bible for guidance and inspiration. Many are
tired of having their faith manipulated and twisted into neat
sound bites, simplistic formulas and narrow wedge issues.
These young people are yearning for a more holistic and active
faith, if the church was only willing to quench their spiritual

hunger with home-cooked meals instead of microwave dinners filled with dogmatic doctrine, spiritual self-help and overly commercialized religion. There are striking similarities between the social and political environment at the beginning of the 1960s and the present age. Young generations in both moments experienced the end of a long prosperity, the election of a young and inspirational president, and the nation's jarring participation in a grossly unjust war with no foreseeable end.

The journey of the transformed nonconformist starts with seeing and making activism a core requirement of discipleship and no longer as an optional or extracurricular activity of faith. Every generation must make a choice. Otherwise, we will become old wine stuck in old wineskins. Old wine misappropriates Jesus' words that the poor will always be among us. Old wine bows to cynicism that our political system is just too broken and accepts partisan gridlock and ideological stalemate as the norm. Old wine blames and scapegoats the poor and oppressed, washing our hands of responsibility as the weak and the marginalized are allowed to remain far too invisible. In old wine, we close our eyes and tighten our fists, walking by people left bruised and battered on the Jericho roads of this nation and world. But new wine unlocks the power God has given us to build a bridge to a different reality. As new wine, young people serve as the moral interrogators and prophetic leaders for social and economic justice. We must pour new ways of thinking and living out our faith, while learning from and building on the old, into new strategies and methodologies for creating social and political change.

Mobilizing hope involves pouring new ideas, new paradigms, new passion, new conviction and new sacrifice into new strategies, new tactics and new methods for change. As a generation, we have the opportunity to redefine and reclaim activism, not according to the cultural wars, doctrinal debates and broken political categories of the past, but according to the redemptive and transforming power of a gospel that is always alive and a God that continually makes all things new. What is needed is a dedicated circle of transformed nonconformists who are committed to remaking the world in the image of God's just kingdom because of and not in spite of their faith.

CHAPTER 1
ACTIVISM IS A STORY OF FAITH

DURING MY SECOND YEAR as a graduate student at the Kennedy School of Government, I took a course titled "Organizing People, Power and Change" with Professor Marshall Ganz. Ganz has been my exacting and tough-minded mentor in community organizing, having spent decades working with Cesar Chavez in the United Farm Workers movement and other similar struggles. In one semester, Ganz opened my eyes to the ways in which organizing people for social change is both an art form and a science. Before taking his course, I was a novice when it came to understanding the nature of power and the architecture of building effective campaigns.

From Ganz I learned that collective action represents the safeguard of our democracy and an antidote to the misuse and abuse of power. I also learned that successful campaigns require much more than the personal charisma of a leader; they also require an understanding of the role that public narrative plays in fueling social change. Too often history is taught in a way that feeds our culture's fixation and fascination with iconic leaders like Dr. King.

This trend renders invisible the unsung heroes who served as the foot soldiers of the civil rights movement. While we remember the oratorical genius of Dr. King, countless people learned to tell their public story in ways that elicited both sacrifice and commitment from others. The use of storytelling or public narrative through countless face-to-face meetings was the lifeblood of recruiting and sustaining participation in bus boycotts, voter registration campaigns and sit-ins.

The first act of becoming creatively maladjusted is to reclaim your own story, which is an act of both empowerment and self-actualization that involves a deliberate process of reflecting on the experiences that have shaped your identity and influenced your life the most. Telling our story, or public narrative, represents the lifeblood of activism. Our public stories are more than simply our testimonies, which describe our personal encounters with God's grace and goodness. Public stories link our personal stories to the stories of others in order to inspire collective action.

According to Ganz, "public narrative is a leadership art through which we translate values into action: engaging heart, head, and hands."[1] Public narrative weaves together Aristotle's three components of rhetoric—logos, pathos and ethos. The logos is the logic of the argument; the pathos is the feeling the argument evokes; and the ethos comes from the credibility of the person who makes the argument. Shocking statistics and compelling facts are almost never enough to inspire people to take action. Personal stories are needed to evoke emotion and trigger empathy.

A good public story is drawn from spiritual markers or choice points that compose the "plot" in our lives. The plot names the challenges we have faced, the choices we have made in the midst of these challenges and the outcomes we've experienced as a result.[2] Choice moments represent footholds that bring our public narrative to life.

Public narrative is composed of three components: a story of self, a story of us and a story of now. The first century sage Rabbi Hillel captured the relationship between these core elements when he said, "If I am not for myself, who is for me? And if I am for myself alone, what then am I? And if not now, then when?"[3] In other words, what are your core values, who constitutes your community and what do you feel so passionate about that you are willing to sacrifice time and energy to change?

The "story of self" is composed of key moments in our lives when our values are formed and we have to choose a course of action in the face of uncertainty.[4] This story is composed of a series of footnotes in our background, upbringing and life experience that form our character, values and convictions. For some of us, our parents play a leading role; for others it may be a grandparent, teacher, neighbor or mentor. Our race, ethnicity, gender and socioeconomic background also play a key role in underwriting this story. While our story of self should never be reduced purely to these attributes, we shouldn't be afraid to articulate the ways in which they've shaped our identity and story.

Why our community, organization, movement and so on has been called to achieve a set of goals forms the "story of us." Community stories include the challenges we have faced collectively and why we stood up to them based on our shared values, religious traditions and political and economic beliefs. We repeat community stories as folk sayings, popular songs, religious rituals and community celebrations, such as Easter, Passover and the Fourth of July.[5] Ganz says that "learning to tell a 'story of us' requires deciding who the 'us' is, which values shape that identity, and which of those values are most relevant to the situation at hand."[6]

Transformed nonconformists can't lose sight of the "us" they are connected to—in some cases making decisions to be connected to one "us" over another, ultimately for the sake of all of us. For instance, Moses chose Israel's story over Egypt's story in accepting God's assignment to free the Israelites from the bondage of slavery.

Like Moses, the "us" for people of faith must always be aligned with God's special concern for the weak, the vulnerable and the marginalized. Therefore, no matter our station in life, our "us" is always inclusive of and concerned about God's chosen "us."

The urgent challenge we are called to face now, the choices we must make to act now and the change we might achieve as a result form the "story of now." The challenge must convey immediacy as we are called upon to act now because of whose we are and the preferred future we aspire to create together. The intersection between the stories of self and us and the pressing injustices in the world gives birth to the story of now. A good story of now breaks us out of inertia and offers an imperative for taking action.

In cases in which we fail to author our own story, others will often fill in the blanks for us. The 2004 presidential campaign of Senator John Kerry provides a haunting example of this in the political realm. The Kerry campaign initially remained silent while a couple of conservative bishops attacked Kerry's Catholic faith due to his pro-choice position, threatening to deny him communion. Thus, this negative storyline became the dominant frame in the media and the public's mind rather than a positive image of Kerry as a devout Catholic believer and churchgoer. The Swift Boat Veterans ads also cast doubts and aspersions upon Kerry's military service. While the campaign had noble reasons for trying to stay above the fray, these negative stories disturbed the narrative, in part because the campaign failed to tell its story as effectively and persuasively as its critics. Authoring our own story starts with identifying the watershed moments in our lives that often determine our trajectory and form our character.

BURNING BUSH MOMENTS

Moses wrestled with the stories of self, us and now in his struggle to accept God's calling upon his life to free the Israelites from the yoke of slavery and lead them into the Promised Land.[7] While we know little about Moses' early life, we do have evidence of his intolerance toward injustice. For example, in Exodus 2, Moses strikes down and kills an Egyptian who he sees brutally beating a Hebrew slave, leading to his forced exile from Pharaoh's court. Moses' dual Egyptian and Hebrew identity enables him to understand the ways and means of Pharaoh's court while also identifying with the oppressed Hebrew slaves. Moses is faced with a painful but conscious choice to either turn a blind eye to oppression and hold on to his life of comfort and privilege, or decide to get in the way of injustice and risk losing everything. Creative maladjustment often means making similar choices, making common cause with the oppressed, and using our status or privilege to fight injustice.

Years later something bizarre and extraordinary happens. God turns Moses' world upside down when he sees the angel of the Lord appear in a flame of fire out of a burning bush. At the burning bush Moses engages in a heated debate with God, asking, Why me? Who is calling me? Why these people? And why now? These questions echo the stories of self, us and now. What I love about Moses is how much we can relate to his response. His initial reaction to God is one of fear and trepidation. Moses asks, "Who am I that I should go to Pharaoh and bring the Israelites out of Egypt?" but God replies, "I will be with you" (Exodus 3:11-12 NRSV). God's reply represents all the reassurance we should need, serving as a reminder that God never leaves nor forsakes us, yet Moses still isn't convinced. He then asks, "If I come to the Israelites and say to them, 'The God of your ancestors has sent me to you,' and they ask me 'What is his name?' what shall I say to them?" (Exodus 3:13 NRSV). God replies, "I am who I am" (Exodus 3:14 NRSV). God reminds Moses that his identity is inextricably linked to his faith. Moses' story of us is bound together with the plight of the Israelites and God's promise to deliver them. In the end, Moses chooses Israel's story over

Egypt's because the twisted logic of Egypt was at odds with God's covenantal promise to Abraham.

When was the last time you experienced a burning bush moment? Typically our burning bushes aren't as dramatic as the one that Moses faced, but there are more subtle moments in our lives when God commands our greatest attention, sometimes in an abrupt instance and other times far more gradually. Burning bush moments are deep encounters with God's will and calling. We may not always see God in the moment, but if we look deep beneath the surface of our experiences, we can see God's presence and purpose become manifest. Burning bush experiences test and try us, stretching our sense of calling and presenting us with crossroad moments.

HOW FAR DOES THE RABBIT HOLE GO?

In a systematic theology course taught by Dr. John Kinney, dean of the Samuel Proctor School of Theology, I was charged with selecting and analyzing any popular movie through a theological lens. Movie watching has never been the same since as I now drive my wife nuts with my post-movie theological commentary. Almost every film is chock-full of theological themes and references. Since theology at its core deals with the human condition, the relationship between people and God, and conceptions of afterlife, evil and sin, almost every film constitutes a treasure chest just waiting to be discovered.

In the first groundbreaking movie of the Matrix trilogy, a computer hacker named Neo is tracked down by Morpheus, the leader of a revolutionary band of freedom fighters on a mission to free humanity from the captivity of machines who have enslaved the world. In the film, Neo appears almost as a Christlike figure, referred to by Morpheus as "the One." One of my favorite scenes is the pivotal moment in which Neo is given a life-altering and paradigm-shattering choice of whether to swallow one of two pills.

With the blue pill he will wake up with his memory of his encounter with Morpheus erased, stuck in a dream-induced existence within the Matrix, which is generated by the machines. With this choice he will remain in a blissful sleep, never having to confront the fact that his current reality is just an illusion. Or he can choose the red pill and according to Morpheus "remain in Wonderland and see how far the rabbit hole goes." In other words, he can join a small group of humans freed from the machines who are waging a campaign to liberate humanity. One path offers comfort and security, even if it is a false one. The other offers incredible risk and danger but leads to true emancipation. Neo chooses the red pill and the rest is cinematic history. We may not face decisions as stark as this one, but even in those more subtle moments in which God offers us the red or blue pill, we must ask ourselves which pill do we swallow?

Over the course of our faith journey, God presents us with many Matrix-like moments. In these watershed moments, we are often confronted by injustice and have to make a deliberate and conscious choice about what to do in response. If you excavate the experiences of your life, I'm confident that you have had at least a few of these life-changing moments. In these choice moments, the scales are removed from our eyes and our community or world suddenly looks different. Jesus also experienced some of these moments in his ministry, like the moment when he overturns the tables of the money changers in the temple (Mark 11:15-18); when he confronts the Pharisees for their hypocrisy by challenging them to cast the first stone toward a woman adulterer (John 8:1-11); when he conquers temptation by the devil after forty days of fasting in the desert (Matthew 4:1-11); or when he refuses to deny his identity as the Son of God when questioned by the Sanhedrin (Mark 14:60-65). These are defining choice moments in Christ's ministry that reveal his true character and mission. These decisions also place Christ on a trajectory toward a destination called Calvary's cross to redeem and save humanity.

Sadly, even after accepting Christ into our lives, many of us continue to choose the blue pill despite the transformational opportunities that God puts in our path. We prefer to live our lives protected by walls of comfort and convenience that separate us from the often bitter realities of pain and suffering that lie just outside our purview. We grow deaf to the cries of the world's dispossessed and disinherited. But true discipleship is akin to choosing the red pill, which enlists us in God's redemptive and liberating purposes in the world. Matrix-like moments form the backbone of our public narrative.

Public narrative helps us make sense of the world and ease the movement from patterned thinking to creative maladjustment and transformed nonconformity. While telling your public narrative may seem like a shameless effort to trumpet your own autobiography, I've experienced the impact this exercise can have in building deeper relationships and forming stronger bonds of community. It has taken me some time, practice and reflection to realize that sharing my story is not about pride, ego or self-aggrandizement but is about sharing the most precious and meaningful parts of myself with others. Authenticity and vulnerability counteract coming across as overly self-promoting or self-serving.

Through the exercise of putting together your public narrative, you get to put together scenes from your life that compose an entire plot. In this case you get to play the leading role, direct the shots and edit the film. I realize that this process can be intimidating and uncomfortable. As much experience as I've gained in public speaking, it wasn't until Ganz pushed me before a Sojourners Training for Change conference in 2008 that I became more accustomed and adept at sharing my story through the medium of public narrative. Sharing my story through this method will hopefully enable and empower you to better tell your story as well.

COMING OF AGE

I grew up believing I was born in the wrong era. The same year that Dr. King's life was tragically cut short, my parents made the controversial decision to get married as an interracial couple. My story, which is drenched in the history of the civil rights struggle, intersects with the challenges facing a post–civil rights generation.

My African American mother, Saundra Taylor, grew up in segregated Louisville, Kentucky, was a classmate of Cassius Clay, later known as Muhammad Ali, and became the only black woman to graduate from Depauw University in her class. She later served as the vice president of student affairs first at Western Washington University and then at the University of Arizona.

My middle name, Russell, comes from my mother's father, who died of a heart attack before I was born. Despite never meeting him, I feel as though Russell is constantly with me as I seek to emulate his commitment to public service when he served as a bridge-builder and civic leader in Louisville, Kentucky. Russell was a humanitarian. He would often paraphrase a poem by James Henry Leigh Hunt called "Abou Ben Adhem," saying, "when I die I want to be remembered because I loved my fellow man." After twenty years of working for the *Louisville Defender* newspaper, my grandfather left to work with a new federally funded program called Urban Renewal. The program helped to relocate disadvantaged people, mostly African Americans, from high-crime and high-drug-use areas to better homes and neighborhoods. It was very controversial and highly political. Most African Americans were suspicious and hostile to the relocation idea. But Russell was very persuasive and effective in reassuring them due to his tremendous people and communication skills. He had a very compassionate heart and worked tirelessly to help people who were disadvantaged. For this reason many people trusted him and would listen to how the program could benefit them. However, dealing with this intense level of conflict and distrust took its toll on him. At the age of fifty-four he had a massive heart attack that he survived, but that left him very weak and unable to continue working. He took a disability leave. Two years later he died from a second massive heart attack.

My father, Christopher Taylor, grew up in white America on a farm outside of Cleveland, Ohio. My dad is not the type who follows convention. He is always looking for a great bargain, negotiating upgrades and taking the path less traveled. I admire his charm, wit, compassion and incredible work ethic, even if I sometimes can't fully appreciate his sense of humor. My dad served as an inspiring and dynamic college professor, having taught courses in psychology to thousands of students over the course of his teaching career.

Part of any story of self is the story of our ancestors and parents. The story of self includes the people who had a particular influence on how we perceive the world and conduct ourselves in it, the people whose decisions had an impact on our birth and upbringing: these people contribute materially to the story that we need to claim for ourselves. Whether your parents, siblings, other relatives, a neighbor, a pastor, a friend, highlighting a few of these people will shed greater light on who was instrumental in shaping and inspiring you. My story begins with a reference to my grandfather Russell because he has had such a profound impact on my life, even if I never had the chance to meet him.

My parents met in a Ph.D. program in psychology at Ohio University. To get a Ph.D. all students had to pass a statistics competency exam. Experimental psychology students like my dad usually had little trouble passing. The clinical students like my mom invariably failed the first time, having to take it as many as five more times to pass the requirement. My mom and Marty, a fellow clinical student, decided to hire my dad as a tutor to try to pass the test. My dad has always possessed a gift as a teacher, able to help people understand what question was being asked and what they needed to do to answer it—not just memorization or proficiency in stuffing numbers into formulas, but getting the concepts and basis for analysis. During the tutoring, despite efforts by Marty to keep them apart, my mom and dad became close friends, and eventually they fell in love. When Mom and Marty took the stat test, they finished first and second. The faculty immediately assumed that they had cheated, especially Mom because of the obvious—she was a clinical student, she was a woman and she was black. My dad was furious. The faculty was a little suspicious of Marty, but they focused on exposing Mom. My dad intervened and challenged them to give her an oral exam. After a lot of politics and hemming and hawing, the faculty was forced to put up or shut up. My mom passed the exam with flying colors, and my dad quickly became her protector and best friend.

When my parents began dating, some of the "concerned" faculty tried to sign my dad up for therapy. A female faculty member invited my dad to lunch. They had already been talked to by family and friends who pleaded with them, "don't sell out your race"; "don't humiliate your family"; "don't ruin your career"; don't, don't, don't. But this professor had a new angle. Don't let his selfishness ruin my mother's life, career and self-respect. My dad thought it was going to be a lunch, not a roast. After she left, almost unconsciously my dad looked down at the paper placemat, which was a map of the United States, Canada and Mexico for children to color. He reached for a crayon and began x-ing out the states where he thought he and my mom would not be able to live together very easily. His eliminations were based on partial knowledge, assumptions and his gut feeling. States across the country continued to fall like dominoes. After about ten minutes he only had Oregon, Washington and British Columbia left, with question marks on California, Colorado, Connecticut and Vermont. Despite the fact that he and my mom had broken off their relationship and my mom had moved to Philadelphia for an internship, he began focusing his job search in the Northwest with this question in mind.

My dad's first interview was at Western Washington University in Bellingham, Washington. The interview went extremely well and he was offered a teaching position; however, his one precondition was that the university also offer my mother a position in the counseling department. He called my mother to share the good news. Surprised to hear from my dad, she replied, "Kit, are you asking me to marry you?" In 1968, my parents decided to place their love over bigotry, getting married in a ceremony that my dad's stepmother refused to accept. Like many others, she had tried to convince my father not to marry my mother. After months and then a year of no baby, my dad's stepmother finally had to consider other reasons behind their marriage. Ironically, her greatest argument against their marriage was me, because, she argued, their children would be casualties of a confused identity with no home or community in which to reside. Little did she know that my multicultural complexion and my biracial background would help me build bridges across the chasm of race and play a key role in inspiring a life-term commitment to social justice. After getting married, my parents moved to Bellingham, Washington, to teach and start a new life together. They taught me to see that every person is made in the image of God and that we are called to celebrate and dignify that diversity. Their example became my first working definition of social justice, rooted in faith and baptized by love.

Stories possess the power to unlock empathy, appeal to shared values and convey deeper meaning than simply a restatement of events, facts or experiences. The story about how my parents fell in love and ultimately got married provides insight into the values they instilled within me and foreshadows how my biracial background inspired my future work for racial reconciliation and justice. This story seeks to set the tone for the rest of my public narrative as someone who doesn't shy away from the realities of social and institutional marginalization and is intimately tied to the spirit of the times but defiantly personal in my creative maladjustment. Somewhere in your background is a story of how someone in your family or ancestry faced and overcame some kind of adversity or challenge. This prehistory tells the story of self and lays the groundwork for the story of us and the story of now.

At the age of fourteen, my conception of the world was enlarged after joining my parents on a two-month trip across Southeast Asia. We traveled across Malaysia, Japan and Thailand during the height of their economic boom and transformation. One memory in Thailand stands out from the others. Pattaya was the southeast capital for military R and R during the Vietnam conflict. The city specialized in "pleasure," every kind of erotic fantasy someone could imagine and more that they could not. The heart of the pleasure district was an eight-block area known to be very dangerous. My parents decided that this area would be off-limits to the family. I protested arguing, "We are in Thailand and should experience every aspect of the country. If we go in the middle of the day, we should be safe." I was persistent and my parents folded. As we walked the streets cautiously, we saw all kinds of propositions, commerce and sleaze. Street after street had doorways, alleyways and windows with young girls in a state of undress exposing their wares through provocative mini-costumes and salacious come-ons. My parents were clearly nervous and uncomfortable. Tears of sadness started running uncontrollably down my face. My parents asked me what was the matter, and I replied, "These young girls are my age, many younger and a few older. Their childhood is being stolen from them. They will never be able to be just kids. They will be scarred forever and that makes me angry." I felt a deep sense of solidarity with these Thai children, realizing that if not for an accident of birth, my childhood could also be stolen by forced prostitution. This incident was a lesson in how capricious life can be, and how abuse and injustice suffocate the potential and rob the future of children.

When I was sixteen years old, my parents uprooted me in the middle of high school and moved our family to Tucson, Arizona, where my mom accepted the prestigious role as the vice president for student affairs at the University of Arizona. Needless to say, at first I was a little bitter. The transition from the temperate climate of the Pacific Northwest to the hundred-degree, sweltering heat of Arizona was a jarring shock to the system. Because there was no high school in our section of town, I had to make a choice about where to attend school anywhere in the city. I knew that the safest and "best" option was to enroll at a predominantly white school for academically advanced students; however, my heart and spirit were pulled elsewhere. I chose a high school that possessed a great deal of socioeconomic and racial diversity. This decision opened the door to greater opportunities to connect with African American culture and began a process of learning more about the culture and experience of Hispanic Americans that continues today.

During my first day of class, I realized that there were two Amphitheater High Schools coexisting under the same roof. My advanced track of classes was almost entirely white and Asian in composition. We benefited from superior resources and gifted teachers that were determined to set us on a path to college. In the other predominantly Latino and black regular track, simply getting students across the threshold of graduation represented the overriding goal. I found myself for the first time at the nexus between students of different racial and socioeconomic backgrounds. Betrayed by this segregation of opportunity, I made it my mission to unite students of color around the shared aspiration of reaching college, regardless of which track they were placed in. I had spent my entire life immersed within a college environment due to my parents' vocations as a professor and an administrator. While going to college was already planted in my DNA, I realized the degree to which this option was undesirable or unobtainable to so many of my peers, particularly my peers of color.

My experiences at Amphitheater High School solidified a belief that education is the passport to a person's future. In our increasingly segregated and unequal education system, education represents the single greatest contributor to persistent and pervasive racial disparities. Through a program designed by the University of Arizona called Academic Preparation for Excellence (APEX), I witnessed firsthand what happens when students of color are given the right kinds of support, encouragement and tools to access higher education. The program formed clubs within middle and high schools focused on fostering academic achievement and college preparation. Through the program I mentored younger students, brought in college advisors and professors, offered free SAT preparation courses and created an environment of positive peer support. While the program could not fully offset the impact of broken homes, unsafe streets, English as a second language and a series of other social and economic barriers that stunt student achievement, it dramatically improved student chances of reaching college. This is not to say that higher education is for every child, but the option must be made real for every child. Hard encounters with the brokenness of our public education system, as well as seeing students triumph despite the odds, later inspired a campaign for educational equity that I launched while serving as the president of the Harvard NAACP chapter called Rallying for Equity and Access to College and Higher Education (REACH).

My family's move to Tucson presented a fairly clear and straightforward choice moment. Ideally the choice moments you identify in your life also possess a degree of tension and risk associated with each choice. These choices also reveal stories of us in the midst of the personal story. For instance, in my decision to attend Amphitheater High School, my "us" became enlarged to include Latino and African American students. In Thailand, my "us" became truly global for the first time, with a deeper concern for children living halfway across the world who had made such an imprint on my consciousness. Creative maladjustment involves expanding our "us" in ways that more closely resemble God's inclusive definition of "us," always identifying with the weak and the marginalized.

A CLOSER WALK WITH GOD

Prior to middle school I had what I now call a "socially correct" faith. My family attended a Presbyterian church on all of the critical religious holidays. However, it wasn't until we joined First Congregational Church in Bellingham, Washington, that I really felt connected to a church and started seriously exploring what it means to a be Christian. The pastor of the church, Reverend Donnell McClellan, was the first minister to make a measurable impact in shaping my faith. Reverend McClellan was both extremely personable and intelligent. His preaching was both practical and intellectual, applying the word of God to moral and ethical questions and to real-life situations. The predominantly white congregational church placed a major emphasis on God's unconditional love and on what it means to live in Christian community. I became extremely active in the church's youth group, representing the church at the National Youth Event in Beloit, Wisconsin, in 1992. I also learned a great deal about Christian fellowship and discipleship through my involvement in Young Life. Yet faith was still much more social than deeply spiritual in nature.

While finishing high school, I became mesmerized with the civil rights era. I read everything I could lay my hands on, from Dr. King's famous speeches and sermons to Taylor Branch's seminal books on Dr. King and the movement. After earning a merit-based scholarship, I decided to attend Emory University in order to trace the origins of the civil rights movement back to the South and experience the predominantly black city of Atlanta, often referred to as a chocolate city.

During my freshman year, I joined Ebenezer Baptist Church,

the spiritual home of Dr. Martin Luther King. The preaching and teaching at Ebenezer echoed themes of black liberation theology, which seamlessly connected faith and social justice. My political and social convictions became grounded in a biblical narrative of justice. After a few visits I responded to an altar call that wasn't only about personal salvation, but also about joining the cause of liberation for the weak and marginalized. I felt as though a major burden had been lifted off my shoulders because I no longer needed to keep my faith at arm's length from a burning call to combat injustice. While at Ebenezer, I learned to appreciate the call and response tradition of the black church, the power of the Holy Spirit expressed through worship and the charismatic preaching style of Dr. Joseph L. Roberts. Ebenezer helped to reinforce my belief that faith is both deeply personal as well as profoundly public and that there is no complete dichotomy between the sacred and the secular.

During my first year of college, Nelson Mandela was elected president of a post-apartheid South Africa. I was euphoric and yearned to see firsthand how South Africa grappled with the struggle for racial reconciliation and justice. I could barely imagine the profound role that South Africa would play in shaping my understanding of social justice. At the time, Emory University didn't sponsor or support study abroad programs outside of Spain and Israel. I petitioned the board and convinced them to make an exception in my case, which later became a precedent for other students. I traveled to South Africa in the winter of 1995, studying at the University of Cape Town through the School for International Training.

While completing an internship in Durban, I was confronted with my own privilege and limitations. I had been thrown into a situation way over my head, teaching conflict resolution skills to a group of young adults older than me. These young people had sacrificed their education to serve as the young lions of the anti-apartheid struggle but felt abandoned by a lack of opportunity in a new South Africa. Their feelings of betrayal and anger made them easy targets for being pulled into political violence. In the process of trying to help them, I started to internalize their pain and had nowhere to channel my own guilt. Instead of turning to God or seeking outside assistance, I fell deeper into a cycle of depression as I tried to mentor these young perpetrators and victims of political violence. Even though they saw me as being capable of showing them a way out of their present condition, I felt powerless given the adverse odds working against them. I ended the internship feeling as though I had failed them.

After the study abroad program ended, I deserted my girlfriend who had traveled across the world to South Africa with a group of Emory students to spend time with me and participate in a service project in Johannesburg. I didn't have the words to confide in her about my struggle, nor could I bring myself to share my battle with depression. It felt easier to simply run away. So in a rash decision, I set off for Zimbabwe with only a backpack to my name. As the week progressed, a deeper loneliness set in. After a week of traveling across what is an awe-inspiring country, I felt led to Victoria Falls, often cited as one of the "seven wonders of the world." As I boarded a bus heading to the falls the only seat left open was next to a beautiful young woman. We talked the entire time heading up to the falls, as though we were long lost friends reunited in a chance encounter. She asked if she could stay with me that night and I said yes. The connection we experienced that night, although not fully consummated, became for me a violation of my girlfriend's trust, accepting solace in the arms of a mysterious woman almost as a replacement for and direct challenge to God. I felt as though not only did I fail a group of young South Africans, I had now failed and would ultimately wound my girlfriend. To make matters worse, I still wasn't able to turn to God for forgiveness, in part because I didn't feel worthy. My perceived fall from grace felt complete.

I awoke the next morning to bursts of lightning, crackling thunder and torrential rain. I walked outside in what felt like a trance, running at full speed in the direction of the falls. As I got closer, the thunderous sound of the falls reverberated in my head. The storm had passed and brilliant rays of sunshine cast rainbows across the canopy of the sky. As I approached the falls I was met by a swirling wall of mist that quickly soaked me to the bone. Then suddenly the mist cleared and the majestic view of cascading water materialized. I fell to my knees with tears streaming down my face. In a state of deep prayer I repented and asked God for forgiveness. At the time I didn't know how to surrender my guilt and feeling of powerlessness to God. But in that poignant moment at the falls, I experienced the power of God's forgiveness and the unmerited gift of God's grace wash over me. I realized that even when we turn away from God, God never turns away from us. I learned that God meets us at our point of weakness and can transform any adversity or situation. The darkness of depression was replaced by the light of God's presence. I felt ready and anxious to join God already at work in the world.

When we share our public narrative our failures, setbacks and moments in the wilderness can teach and reveal as much as our successes and triumphs. These stories play a key role in humanizing us and making our story more accessible and real. In the context of the church, we often call this our testimony. Every testimony starts with a test, something that challenges and stretches us. As transformed nonconformists we will experience our fair share of these moments. The key is to learn how to unearth and communicate the ways in which you are able to turn these situations around. What change in attitude or perspective was necessary? Being creatively maladjusted comes with the realization that we are finite people of conscience whose will has been compromised to one degree or another by sin, feelings of inadequacy or both. Fortunately we serve a God who continually calls, renews, empowers and ultimately sends. My time in South Africa helped me to embrace my own limitations and to recognize that I couldn't conquer the crisis facing many South African youth.

RESISTING A CALL TO MINISTRY

After graduating from college, my struggle with accepting a call to ministry began with greater force. While having been accepted to the Kennedy School of Government at Harvard University, I decided to defer graduate school in order to take a break from academic life and experience a change of pace by working in New York City government through the Urban Fellows program. At least that is what I told myself. In reality I was lost, running away from myself and a deeper commitment to my faith. Emory University had conferred upon me the highest honor given to any graduating student, the Marion Britain Award for exemplary service to the university, the city of Atlanta and the world. In the midst of feelings of pride and gratification was an impenetrable emptiness. I had spent the last few months of my senior year involved in a number of casual relationships and drank more in those short months than I had in my entire college career combined. Church had become an afterthought. I was running away from facing and discerning what God had in store for me. To put an exclamation point on my estrangement, the Dalai Lama served as our graduation speaker. As I arose to accept the Britain award the Dalai Lama stood up and gave me the most humbling bow to show his respect and offer his congratulations.

During my first few months in New York City, I felt as though I had been shipwrecked in a tumultuous sea of frenetic, around-the-clock activity. For someone with almost no sense of direction, New York posed a true test of nerves and patience. Despite the logical gridlike layout of the city, I was constantly getting lost, perhaps almost by design, as my physical disorientation mirrored my spiritual disorientation.

The Urban Fellows program provides recent college graduates an opportunity to work for a year in New York City government through a placement in an agency or the mayor's office. The program also provides exposure into city politics through a series of weekly seminars and excursions. I knew entering the program that I didn't agree with much of Mayor Giuliani's politics; however, I wanted to have my beliefs and thinking stretched. Over the course of the year, it became more and more difficult to reconcile the mayor's increasingly heavy-handed and autocratic governing style, particularly in response to alarming cases of alleged police brutality. The most egregious case was of Amadou Dialo, a West African immigrant who was shot forty-one times by police officers while standing innocently outside his home. The incident set off a firestorm of protest across the city.

In the midst of this tumultuous political environment, I searched for spiritual meaning and truth. I felt God's pull on my life and I knew that God wanted a more personal and intimate relationship. Faith had often been an overly intellectual exercise in my life. Jesus could have some areas of my life but not all of me. By giving only a part of myself to God, I was essentially left broken.

Only two blocks from my apartment complex in Brooklyn I discovered a dynamic and vibrant Baptist church called Emmanuel Baptist. The pastor, Anthony Trufant, preached from within the African American cultural tradition, weaving themes of empowerment, liberation, and personal and communal responsibility into his sermons. Emmanuel was a very Afrocentric church that celebrated the uniqueness and richness of African, Caribbean and African American culture in the context of worship and ministry.

Emmanuel Baptist Church exposed me to the fruits of a small-group ministry that met on Wednesday evenings. Initially I joined a group composed of all black women who were literally matriarchs within their community. We used the Willow Creek Following God series to explore the core tenets of the Christian faith. I now realize how haughty and incredulous I must have come across in those initial classes. I concealed my doubts and fears under a layer of bombast and overconfidence, questioning everything and pretending that I possessed the answers to faith's most enigmatic questions. Ruth, the facilitator of the group, saw right through my facade and kindly but firmly took me under her spiritual mentorship. She taught me to see how my misguided self-sufficiency had become a dangerous crutch. Keeping God at arm's length was literally tearing me apart.

As I began to let God into all of my life, my attitude toward the Fellows program, my job and New York City made a 180-degree turn. Where I once felt overwhelmed, I now felt energized and stimulated. I even felt empowered to challenge some of the mayor's policies that I found most objectionable, leading discussions around racial justice with other participants in the Urban Fellows program. After switching to a small group designed for young adults, my gifts in ministry started to shine. Within four months, Pastor Trufant asked me to serve as the leader of the church's young adult ministry. I questioned whether I was biblically qualified for the role, but accepted anyway, stepping out in faith. While leading the group, God continually laid biblical insights and encouragement upon my heart. As the year progressed, I started feeling a greater pull into ministry. Pastor Trufant also sensed this calling and asked whether I should be going to divinity school instead of the Kennedy School of Government for a public policy degree.

I entered graduate school with this question of where God was calling me to go still swirling around in my spirit. As I combed the course guide looking to choose my one elective class for the fall one unorthodox course description stood out from the others. Rev. Jim Wallis, the founder of Sojourners, was offering a course on the intersection between faith and politics. I confess that at that point in my life I had never heard of Rev. Wallis or of Sojourners, but one of the students that I had already met through the Christian fellowship said that the course was a match made in heaven for my interests. She was right; the course represented an oasis in an otherwise highly secular Harvard environment, helping me to further connect the dots between my faith and politics. I was able to learn more about the role of faith in social reform and social movements and examine the impact of religion in American politics.

Creative maladjustment becomes rooted in our relationships and is nearly impossible in isolation. Thus, our commitment is sustained and nourished by our spiritual confidantes and a worshiping community. Mentors like Rev. Jim Wallis and Pastor Jeffrey Brown played instrumental roles in inspiring and encouraging my transformed nonconformity. I want you to identify in your life mentors and confidantes who have helped you recognize and better use your gifts.

Around this same time I joined Union Baptist Church in Cambridge. The motto of the church is to be a "lighthouse unto the community." I was drawn to the pastor's leadership and commitment to making ministry relevant beyond the four walls of the church by reaching at-risk youth. Reverend Jeffrey Brown was a cofounder of the Boston Ten Point Coalition, an initiative started in 1996 by black clergy determined to take back the streets of Boston from violence and fear. After a spate of teen violence, a group of urban ministers believed that if they did not take the gospel to the streets, violence would overtake the church. Reverend Brown tackled social and political issues, helping me understand that accepting a call into ministry did not require compartmentalizing my passion for politics and social justice. After deciding to spend a summer in Zambia working on HIV/AIDS prevention programs, Rev. Brown recommended that I read the entire Bible as well as two devotionals by Henry Fosdick titled *The Meaning of Prayer* and *The Meaning of Service*.

While in Zambia I woke up at the crack of dawn to read the New Testament with new eyes and greater vigor, from the Gospel of Matthew to the book of Revelation. I decided to put God to the test, expecting God to speak from the heavens with an epiphany that would erase my inner tension between accepting a call into ministry and pursuing a career in social justice. Despite these morning devotions and rigorous Bible study, I had yet to receive the revelation about ministry that I was searching for. I was still hoping for a burning-bush moment in which God would give me a sense of certainty around a call into ministry.

As my internship came to a close, I decided to use my final week to travel to Tanzania in order to climb Mt. Kilimanjaro. I was convinced that the grueling hike to the peak of this awesome mountain would get me closer to God and to the answer that I had been seeking. Normally the hike takes a full five days to complete, but due to time and money constraints I recklessly attempted to complete it in three days. Starting in a lush jungle, I made a steady climb winding up into the heavens. I traveled through grassland, savannah, tundra and finally snow, reaching an elevation of over eighteen thousand feet. The first day was exhilarating as we reached the point at which we were walking through the clouds. By the second day, altitude sickness hit my body like a flood. I couldn't hold down any food and had a dangerously high fever. I stumbled to the final rest stop, barely able to put one foot in front of the other. But I was determined and convinced that God would speak to me at the top of the mountain. A Swedish doctor pleaded with me not to set off for the summit after taking my temperature and seeing that I had a 103-degree fever.

Instead of following her instructions, I set off for the summit in an act of foolhardy desperation with only the moonlight illuminating the way, taking an unnecessary risk with my life. After three hours of hiking I collapsed out of total exhaustion. I literally had nothing left. Upon hitting the ground I entered into a deep meditation in which I was filled with an incredible sense of God's presence. In this deep meditative state I had a heated argument with

God, asking, "Why have you led me all the way to this point only to forsake me now?" God's response was simple and direct: "I didn't lead you up here; you did." Sometimes we can take ourselves far too seriously. God showed me in that instant that the answer I had been seeking to find through divine intervention or some kind of miracle had been within me the entire time. The irreconcilable tension between a call to ministry and a call to social justice was replaced by a calm conviction that the two were inextricably linked. After regaining consciousness, I felt an incredible sense of peace about my call to ministry. I turned around and started the descent down the mountain. Within hours the fever lifted, my strength returned and my soul felt exalted.

MY BURNING BUSH MOMENT

I experienced a seminal burning bush moment during the first International AIDS Conference to take place on African soil in Durban, South Africa, in 2000. During the course of my first year at the Kennedy School in 1999, the harrowing and sobering statistics surrounding the AIDS pandemic were just breaking into the mainstream press and public consciousness. Already a flurry of activity was taking place across Harvard University through the activism of economist Jeffrey Sachs, the research of the Harvard AIDS Institute and the innovative and groundbreaking clinical work of Partners in Health in Haiti, which sought to provide AIDS treatment to people living in extreme poverty. The harrowing statistics of AIDS assaulted my conscience and stoked my outrage around how the world could watch and allow this human emergency to unfold.

I decided that I needed to see what was happening firsthand, beyond the paralyzing statistics, so I secured a grant to work for the summer with a development organization called Africare in Zambia. After a month of working alongside Zambian youth to strengthen HIV prevention programs, I arrived in Durban for the International AIDS Conference, which focuses the world's attention on the epidemic every two years. The conference was taking place at the epicenter of the pandemic in Kwa-Zulu Natal, a region in which an estimated 30 percent of the adult population was already living with HIV. The conference title "Breaking the Silence" was fitting given the conspiracy of silence, stigma and denial that surrounded the epidemic in South Africa and around the world. During the opening ceremony, President Thabo Mbeki gave a thirty-minute speech without ever uttering the words HIV or AIDS, in large part because he was still in denial that HIV in fact causes AIDS. It was a surreal moment in which the negligent leadership of the South African government was on full display.

The next day during the opening plenary, Judge Edwin Cameron gave an electrifying speech that felt like a burning bush moment. Judge Cameron was a white South African judge who had gone public with his HIV positive status at a great risk to his career. He described to an audience of over ten thousand researchers, doctors, public health workers and activists how just months prior to the conference he had been on his deathbed. His immune system had been weakened by the virus and his body looked emaciated. I was already moved by his passionate testimony but was unprepared for what came next. The cadence and volume of his voice ratcheted up a notch as he said, "My presence here embodies the injustice of AIDS because, on a continent in which 290 million Africans survive on less than one U.S. dollar a day, I can afford medication costs of about $400 a month."[8] Because of his wealth, his skin color and his status in South African society, he was able to pay for life itself. He could purchase life-prolonging medicines called antiretroviral drugs that literally brought him from the brink of death back to life, creating what many now refer to as the Lazarus effect. But AIDS still represented a deadly and brutal death sentence for the vast majority of the world, including the majority of his black South African brothers and sisters living with the virus. I felt as though a semi-truck had collided with my notion of justice and equality. HIV made the inequalities of this world burn in living color. The moral failure of our increasingly globalized world hung in the air like a suffocating fog.

The conference was a turning point in the global movement to fight HIV/AIDS, shining a spotlight on pharmaceutical greed, political denial, societal stigma and a global failure to address what had already become the single greatest health crisis in human history. Conventional political and public health wisdom at the time argued that AIDS drugs were simply too expensive, that African countries lacked the health infrastructure to deliver the drugs safely and effectively and that prolonging lives with expensive treatments wasn't cost effective or sustainable. After the conference I decided to join a committed minority of nonconformists who refused to accept these arguments. We walked away having swallowed the red pill, determined to break the silence around the epidemic and see how far the rabbit hole would take us until the AIDS epidemic was reversed.

I returned to Boston for my second year at the Kennedy School on a mission to share my experience with as many people as would listen. I framed the AIDS epidemic as a crisis that exposed and was driven by a series of injustices and a great deal of brokenness within the human condition. In other words, the world couldn't truly stop the AIDS epidemic without also addressing stigma, drug abuse, poverty, gender inequality, violence against women, homophobia and sexual behavior. Working closely with Dr. Jeffrey Sachs, I received a seed grant to start a nonprofit organization to educate and mobilize college students around issues of global economic and social justice. Our first campaign focused on ending the AIDS pandemic through the Student Global AIDS Campaign (SGAC). SGAC joined a burgeoning movement of people living with HIV, public health advocates and many faith leaders working to generate public pressure and to sound the alarm for Congress and the Clinton then Bush administrations to wake up to the crisis and provide bolder

leadership in response. Through letter-writing campaigns, lobbying, op-eds and demonstrations, college students from across the
country made fighting AIDS a "cause of their generation." This
groundswell of activism spurred the creation of the Global Fund to
Fight AIDS, TB and Malaria and the groundbreaking announcement by President Bush in 2002 of the Presidential Emergency Plan
for AIDS Relief (PEPFAR). Seven years later the number of people
in the developing world receiving life-prolonging antiretroviral
drugs went from a shameful fifty thousand in 2001 to over three
million in 2008. Public pressure forced the cost of a year's worth of
AIDS drugs down over the same period from roughly $15,000 per
person per year to less than $300 a person per year for generic
versions.

At the 2008 International AIDS conference in Mexico City, Dr.
Peter Piot, head of UNAIDS, declared that "for the first time,
fewer people are dying of AIDS and fewer people are becoming
infected with HIV. For the first time, we have empirical evidence
that our brilliant coalition can move mountains."[9] This revolution
in treatment access would not have been possible without the tireless advocacy and relentless organizing efforts of a global campaign fighting AIDS. This is just one of the many hopeful examples of modern day campaigns that have generated remarkable
change. In the movement to end AIDS I experienced firsthand the
power of activism. Coming out of the 2000 AIDS conference, I
was confident that I was walking in God's purpose. The HIV/
AIDS crisis intersected with my passion for social justice and conviction that because young people were disproportionately affected, they must serve on the vanguard of turning the epidemic
around.

There are explosive moments when our life's journey corre-
sponds with the painful story of the world we inhabit. In these
moments we cease imagining and begin resolving that God has
been leading us through the discreet chapters of our life toward a

particular role in the unfolding story of God's people. Our story of self and our story of us coalesce in a story of now, a kind of *kairos* that only an all-seeing, all-loving God could have composed.

Kairos moments are those moments in which the arc of time is controlled by the hand of God. I learned during my travels in South Africa that *kairos* moments are preceded by times in which the present reality becomes so fraudulent and pernicious that new vision and bold action is required. In these moments, the old patterns we've hummed along to feel oddly discordant. The way forward seems as clear to us as it does counterintuitive to the ways of the world. Our story of now has a new plot and a greater purpose inspired by a God who has been ordering our steps all along. At an explosive moment like this we discover that we are something new, creatively maladjusted and spoiled for the status quo. We have the moral imagination to see a reversal in the HIV/AIDS epidemic and the boldness to take on a crisis of this magnitude in our midst. We discover that we are called to be God's change agents, empowered by the Holy Spirit to be God's transformed nonconformists.

CHAPTER 2
GETTING TO THE ROOT CAUSE OF INJUSTICE

SOCIAL JUSTICE HAS GROWN increasingly en vogue. Fortunately, many of the former battle lines between the evangelical fixation with personal salvation and the mainline protestant emphasis on social action is fading thanks to a growing hunger for a more holistic gospel that embraces both a personal relationship with God and an active faith engaged in God's purposes in this world. Yet the term *social justice* is often used rather loosely, taking on a broad spectrum of often conflicting meanings. Social justice easily becomes a catch all term that loses its specificity and power. In some cases, one person's definition of justice represents another person's sense of injustice. For example, in the highly contentious debate around abortion, pro-life advocates argue that they are protecting the rights and lives of unborn children while many pro-choice proponents contend they are protecting the rights and health of women. Both sides believe justice is on their side and often appeal to protecting human dignity and rights.

People of faith often mischaracterize their acts of charity and compassion as acts of justice. I've often asked many churches whether they are engaged in social justice and they often proudly describe ministries in which their members visit the imprisoned, feed the homeless and care for the elderly. These are all beautiful expressions of Christian love, compassion and hospitality but are very different than biblical justice, which seeks to advance communal righteousness rather than simply personal righteousness. An October 2008 Barna Group survey of 1,024 Protestant and Catholic pastors nationwide found that while 80 percent supported missionaries overseas and 69 percent sent financial aid to respond to a natural disaster, only 12 percent had worked to change government or business policies that are unfair to the poor in other countries.[1]

The Bible is clear that compassion is part of our calling as the people of God, but advancing justice is also part of our calling and clearly distinct in its character. Biblical justice seeks to redress the root causes behind people's need and pain. Biblical justice continues to ask the question "why" until these root causes are unearthed and addressed. Charity often provides a short-term fix by helping people with their immediate needs, yet it often fails to remove the source of exploitation or oppression that violates their dignity and keeps them in need. An obvious and blatant example of this distinction was in the case of Jim Crow segregation in the South. Many white churches responded with acts of compassion to the plight of African Americans, yet no volume of charity could reverse their political disenfranchisement and economic subordination. Justice required both new laws and the enforcement of existing laws, matters that required policy and systemic change.

In a more contemporary example, charity provides critical help to a single mother working full time in a minimum wage job trying to provide for her kids. While charity provides her with a leg up, it fails to provide a leg out of poverty. Justice demands a way out of poverty, which involves higher wages and greater access to affordable health care and childcare so the mother doesn't have to make

a choice between caring for her kids and trying to make a livelihood. Charity mentors a child who lags behind in test scores, often
because they are stuck in a failing or inadequate school. However,
justice demands reforms to our education system to ensure that
every child receive a quality education in the first place. Charity
can provide counseling and job training to inmates, an alarming
percentage of which were wrongfully convicted. Justice demands
that the wrongfully convicted are exonerated and that the criminal
justice system is reformed to prevent wrongful convictions from
occurring in the first place.

Unfortunately, justice and compassion often get pitted against
each other, creating a false choice between them. The prophet Isaiah resolves this false dichotomy in the fifty-eighth chapter of Isaiah. Isaiah is addressing Israel in roughly 540 B.C., forty-five years
after the destruction of Judah and Jerusalem by the Babylonian
Empire and the deportation of many Jews to Babylon. In this text,
Isaiah speaks against the dangers of superficial ritual as a substitute for real justice and mercy. In this case, the cultic ritual of fasting is worthwhile only insofar as it advances our identification as
the people of God, which manifests itself as loving mercy and doing justice, to borrow from another prophet, Micah. To the degree
that rituals become a pattern, they can become a barrier to our
discipleship and no longer serve as an act of devotion.

Isaiah 58 begins by asking what kind of fasting God seeks from
God's followers. Isaiah says, "Is not this the kind of fasting I have
chosen: to loose the chains of injustice and untie the cords of the
yoke," and goes on to say "Is it not to share your food with the
hungry and to provide the poor wanderer with shelter—when you
see the naked, to clothe him, and not to turn away from your own
flesh and blood?" (Isaiah 58:6-7). In this passage, people fast and
see it as a righteous act; however, Isaiah rejects fasting that is disconnected from works of compassion and justice. Genuine compassion for the poor and the oppressed is deemed more important

than purely correct worship or sound doctrine. God prefers acts of righteousness that overturn the injustice afflicting the downtrodden over pious worship that has no bearing on loving and protecting our neighbor. Isaiah is also warning us not to let our religious acts and forms of worship devolve into a purely private and personal enterprise.

Isaiah goes on to say that the livelihood and spiritual health of the people of God is tied to the liberation of the downcast and downtrodden among them. After we've engaged in acts of compassion and justice, Isaiah says, "Then your light shall break forth like the dawn, and your healing shall spring up quickly" (Isaiah 58:8 NRSV). The text is clear that healing is not limited to those who are hungry and homeless but includes those who have bread and space to share. In other words, in Isaiah's vision it is not some people healing other people. Instead, we all get healed. Isaiah ends this extraordinary text saying: "The LORD will guide you continually, and satisfy your needs in parched places, and make your bones strong; and you shall be like a watered garden, like a spring of water, whose waters never fail. Your ancient ruins shall be rebuilt; you shall raise up the foundations of many generations; you shall be called the repairer of the breach, the restorer of streets to live in" (Isaiah 58:11-12 NRSV). I love this image of people being used by God to become repairers of the breach and restorers of streets to live in.

This text reinforces that it is counterproductive and unnecessary to pit justice and charity against each other, particularly because both are part and parcel to building God's kingdom. In reality, charity and justice reinforce each other. Seeking justice without an orientation of charity can devolve into self-righteousness and cultural imperialism. I will pick up this theme later, but advocacy on behalf of others that isn't steeped in real relationship loses its legitimacy and moral compass. On the other hand, charity without a commitment to justice is a palliative but almost never a cure. At worst, charity without a commitment to justice can turn into paternalism and lead to an unhealthy cycle of dependency. People are often much more comfortable writing a check or giving to a mission offering that feeds the hungry, heals the sick and shelters the homeless than advocating for policies and programs that will prevent hunger, extend health care coverage and combat homelessness.

The difference between social justice and charity is real and must be better understood in order for us to live out the entire gospel. Using the familiar adage, charity is giving a man or woman a fish to eat for a day. Justice is not only teaching them how to fish, but also working to ensure that they can own the pond and that the pond doesn't become polluted by outside forces. In this case, teaching them how to fish is still necessary but almost never enough. Using another common adage, charity is pulling children out of harm's way who have been thrown into a turbulent stream while justice is going upstream to stop whatever is throwing them in. In this case, charity represents the first and necessary response. You can't leave the children to drown while you go upstream to figure out the root cause of what's causing them to be in danger. At the same time, you can't simply pull endless kids out without going upstream to address the root cause of what's throwing them in.

JUSTICE AND SILLY PUTTY

Justice can be a slippery concept to define. Do you remember silly putty, that forever malleable substance that you used to play with as a kid to mold and shape into almost anything your imagination could conceive? Justice often feels like silly putty. The question of how we should live together has shaped considerations of a just society throughout human history. For instance, Greek aristocrats taught the ethic "to everyone his due." The philosophical concept of utilitarianism measures morality by what will maximize "the greatest happiness for the greatest number." Liberalism places a premium on "individual autonomy" and choice. Kant gave us the principle of treating every person as an end in themselves and never only as a means. The great political theorist John Rawls defined "social justice" simply as the collective, negotiated embodiment of the basic human understanding of "fairness."[2]

Professor Michael Sandel, who teaches a famous course at Harvard University on justice, writes that "to ask whether a society is just is to ask how it distributes the things we prize—income and wealth, duties and rights, powers and opportunities, offices and honors."[3] Sandel synthesizes volumes of political theory and ethics into three primary ways of approaching justice through the goals of welfare, freedom and virtue. Debate about justice often centers on maximizing welfare by promoting prosperity and improving standards of living. Theories of freedom emphasize respect for individual rights, even though theorists often disagree about which rights are most important. The freedom school is often divided into the laissez-faire camp, who believe that justice consists in respecting and upholding the voluntary choices made by consenting adults, and the fairness camp, who argue that justice requires policies that remedy social and economic disadvantages and give everyone a fair chance at success. Finally, there are theories that see justice as being bound up with notions of virtue and what constitutes the "good life."[4]

While there are real merits to studying and applying each of these approaches to justice, these secular definitions often fail to go far enough. Secular definitions tend to start with the question of how we should live instead of the question, "To whom do we belong and give account?" The Bible provides a more holistic definition of justice rooted in notions of shalom, righteousness and God's kingdom come. Reverend Aaron Graham[5] believes that "biblical justice is living out your Kingdom come on earth as it is in Heaven. It is seeking God's shalom, or completeness, in areas of society that are broken and working toward reconciling all things

back to God's original intention."[6] By extension this means that for
Dr. King, who was first and foremost a Baptist preacher, simply
securing legal civil rights protections was not enough; the kingdom of heaven on earth demanded that the beloved community be
built. Dr. King refused to embrace violent means for achieving political victories for civil rights because unjust means corrupt just
ends. Nonviolent social protest became both the method and the
philosophy for building the beloved community, all based in an
ethic that only love could conquer enmity and hatred. For Desmond Tutu, the end of apartheid was merely a step along the way
to a new "rainbow nation" in South Africa. Tutu had the faith and
foresight to understand that getting there required the painful but
transformative work of the Truth and Reconciliation Commission
to uncover the truth about apartheid's atrocities and create a platform for forgiveness to take center stage, helping to heal many of
the deep-seated scars left over from the past.

Social justice is a description of an ideal reality in which every
person's dignity and rights are respected and a process by which
we live into that ideal reality. Meanwhile, social injustice is a reality characterized by division, conflict, violence and strife.[7] In a socially just society and world, everyone would work together to put
an end to exploitation, social marginalization and discrimination.
A perfectly just society will always be just out of reach until God's
kingdom is fully consummated. However, Christians should constantly stand out for their tireless pursuit of the ideal.

Justice is about both the end goal we seek to create as well as the
process we pursue in getting there. Another aspiring transformed
nonconformist, Doug Shipman,[8] emphasizes the process around
achieving a more just society, which involves "the continual protection and care for the most vulnerable; an openness and inclusion of diverse opinions and people in a way that provides equal
footing for all, which has ramifications for language, process, time
and understanding; continually developing an empathy for those

most unlike yourself by gender, sexuality, culture, ethnicity, religion, etc."[9] Shipman takes it upon himself to understand others and defend others because he believes "you are who you defend and love." While achieving social justice is often painful, loud and full of conflict, the destination should be the opposite: peaceful, loving and filled with joy.

OLD TESTAMENT BASIS FOR SOCIAL JUSTICE

The Bible defines a just society and world as one in which righteousness, steadfast love and right relationships reign supreme. In both the Old and New Testament, a holy matrimony exists between justice and righteousness, as well as between holiness and doing the work of God's kingdom. Chris LaTondress argues that

> social justice aims at bringing the world into greater alignment with God's best hopes and dreams. For example, in Scripture we discover 2,000 verses revealing God's concern for the poor that are too often hidden in plain sight. We see prophets holding rulers accountable for how they structure political and economic life. Most significantly, we witness a 1st century rabbi who started a revolutionary movement that rejected violence and renounced empire. Through Jesus we are rediscovering the radical (and ancient) idea that when God became flesh he joined peasants rather than kings, exposing the ultimate irrelevance of the powerful, and revealing his love for humanity at its most vulnerable.[10]

Stated in its simplest form, a just society is one in which every person, made in God's image, is able to realize their God-given potential. Inherent in this definition is the understanding that every person is made in the image of God. This can sometimes sound cliché but if we could only learn to take this fully to heart. Thus, when we see another person, we are staring at a reflection of God. Made in God's image or *imago Dei* means that human life is sacred and that every person has equal dignity and worth. Anything that assaults, undermines or distorts that dignity or worth is a form of injustice. This definition ties together notions of human agency, rights, responsibilities and opportunities. Realizing our full, God-given potential requires having access to opportunities that enable these gifts to flourish. Enjoying basic civil and human rights enables us to exercise agency. With these rights come responsibilities to advance the common good.

In his work *On Human Dignity: Political Theology and Ethics*, the great German theologian Jürgen Moltmann outlines a strong, persuasive theological foundation for the ecumenical church's work on human rights tied to the notion of human dignity. Moltmann makes clear his conviction that God's faithfulness to creation is the heart of human dignity. Moltmann argues that human dignity requires human rights for its embodiment, protection and full flowering, and these rights are grounded in God's creation of the human being in God's image. Moltmann writes, "The human rights to life, freedom, community, and self-determination mirror God's claim upon persons, because in all their relationships in life . . . they are destined to reflect the image of God."[11]

Part of the problem is that we miss seeing many references to justice in the Old and New Testament due to overly restrictive translations of the text. By a conservative count, the four words for justice (two in Hebrew and two in Greek) appear 1,060 times in the Bible. The noun *mishpat* appears 422 times in the Hebrew Bible, and it comes from the verb *shapat,* which means to govern and judge."[12] Righteousness is often translated from the Hebrew word *tsedeq* and *tsedaqah*. The feminine version of *tsedaqah* appears 157 times and the masculine version *tsedeq* appears 119 times. Somehow we have overly personalized and privatized the definition of righteousness, when in reality its biblical meaning is much more communal in nature. *Tsedaqah* often means norm or the way things ought to be.[13]

The words justice *(mishpat)* and righteousness *(tsedaqah)*, refer not only to fair legal systems but also to just economic structures. The words very often appear together in Hebrew parallelism, as in Amos 5:24 (NRSV): "Let justice roll down like waters, and righteousness like an ever-flowing stream." Again and again, the biblical texts say: the Lord "has made you king to execute justice and righteousness" (1 Kings 10:9 NRSV; see also Jeremiah 22:15-16).[14]

THE KINGDOM OF GOD AND THEMES OF INJUSTICE

Concepts of justice in the New Testament are inextricably tied to an understanding of the kingdom of God. The kingdom of God serves as a central motif describing Christ's mission and witness to the world. Jesus began his ministry announcing that the kingdom of God was at hand (Mark 1:15). The kingdom becomes both a future event and a present reality. God's reign is inaugurated in Jesus Christ, even if its ultimate consummation remains a future event.[15] While God has already won final victory over the kingdom of the world through Jesus' death on the cross, this victory is not yet fully realized until the kingdom of the world becomes once more the kingdom of our Lord and God's reign is made complete. God seeks to enlist us in the project of building God's kingdom, enabling disciples to get a foretaste of the joy of kingdom living. The kingdom is characterized by "shalom," which includes social justice, peace and righteousness.

In *Kingdom Ethics*, Glen Stassen and David Gushee outline four themes of injustice that Jesus addressed through his teachings and witness. Each theme echoes the prophet Isaiah, the book of Psalms and, to a lesser degree, Genesis and Deuteronomy, including unjust economic structures, unjust domination, unjust violence and unjust exclusion from community. Each represents both a type of injustice and a root cause behind injustice.[16] As we examine and excavate injustices locally and globally we will find these root causes in different degrees and combinations.

First, Jesus addressed the injustice of greed and exploitation. Jesus' most dramatic confrontation with exploitation takes place in Mark 11, when he enters the temple and, in a radical and provocative act, overturns the tables of the money changers. Jesus has just made his triumphal entry into Jerusalem on what we now celebrate as Palm Sunday, riding into the city on a donkey as the people proclaim, "Hosanna in the highest." Jesus' next public act is to enter the temple, where he sees money changers conducting their business and merchants selling doves. In the time of Jesus, the temple operated as the central bank, a place of commerce in which money changers collected interest and fees for the exchange and borrowing of money. During the time of Passover it was common for money changers and merchants to do big business in the temple, often charging inflated exchange rates. Religious leaders would also sell doves at an exorbitant price to be used as religious sacrifices. Jesus' righteous anger is directed both at the temple being defiled by commerce and at commerce that exploits God's people. Jesus quotes the prophet Jeremiah, saying, "Is it not written, 'My house shall be called a house of prayer for all the nations'? But you have made it a den of robbers" (Mark 11:17 NRSV). Jesus' words are revealing. To be robbed means that someone is being abused or that something is being stolen by force or deception. Therefore, the cleansing of the temple becomes a prophetic and symbolic attack on the whole temple system for practicing injustice—the same kind of confrontation offered by both Isaiah 56 and Jeremiah 7.[17]

I often wonder how Jesus would confront modern-day forms of greed and exploitation, whether sweatshop labor, illegitimate and odious debt owed by countries in the Global South to wealthy countries and multilateral banks, modern forms of usury such as payday loans, or the reckless speculation and profiteering that spurred the 2008 global financial collapse. While significant progress has been made thanks to greater public awareness, a great deal of the clothes we wear and products we purchase are still produced under inhumane and intolerable "sweatshop" conditions around the world. These include unsafe work environments, excessive work hours, the exploitation of child labor and brutality toward workers. Many countries accumulated a great deal of unsustainable debt under the auspices of the Cold War, taking out loans that were rarely used for their original purpose and instead lined the pockets of corrupt and dictatorial governments. Despite having paid off the equivalent of the principal, many countries are still paying off these debts due to compound interest—spending more money on debt financing than on health care for their people. Payday loan centers have become almost as common as liquor stores in most inner-city neighborhoods, charging outrageous interest rates on short-term loans. The 2008 financial collapse was precipitated by an overvalued and overheated housing market driven by subprime mortgages and bundled loans. Profit-maximization became the primary end, even if the means of excessive risk taking and speculation placed the entire economy at risk.

We can combat these contemporary forms of exploitation through the power of our consumer choices and political and economic pressure. For instance, transnational corporations rely upon the credibility and integrity of their brand to sell their products. Thus, campaigns that tarnish their image and change consumer behavior represent a significant threat. The campaign around conflict diamonds provides a recent example in which consumer activism was successful in reforming the way in which a major industry conducts its business. As Kanye West sings, "diamonds are forever" and have resulted in a lucrative business with potentially destructive consequences. Global Witness's "Combating Conflict Diamonds" campaign, which was launched in 1998, exposed the role of diamonds in funding conflicts in places like Sierra Leone and the Congo. The campaign put the diamond industry, previously shrouded in secrecy, into the international spotlight, demanding that governments and the diamond industry take action to eliminate the trade in conflict diamonds. In response, in May 2000, the major diamond trading and producing countries, representatives of the diamond industry and NGOs met in Kimberley, South Africa, to determine how to tackle the conflict diamond problem. The meeting was the start of an important and often contentious three-year negotiating process to establish the Kimberley Process, an international diamond certification scheme.[18] A concerted public campaign by a coalition of NGOs successfully exposed the nefarious connection between diamond companies and bloody conflicts, compelling companies to put in place more stringent standards and monitoring systems.

Second is the root cause of domination and powerlessness. Jesus was a poor Jew living within the context of Roman occupation and oppression. Jesus' words and actions must be understood within this oppressive context; otherwise, we can lose the deeper meaning and significance behind his parables and teachings, and we risk over-sanitizing the more radical implications of Jesus' words. One illustration of why we must get underneath the meaning of Jesus' words is the story in Mark 5 in which Jesus exorcises the unclean spirit called "Legion." At the time Jesus lived, "legion referred to none other than the Roman legions, the powerful and brutal Roman army occupying Israel. What is commonly viewed as purely an exorcism turns out to also be a parable indicting the Roman military for its oppression and devastating impact on the social fabric of Israel."[19] Taking Jesus' words out of this context is like trying to understand Dr. Martin Luther King's "I Have a Dream" speech without the backdrop of Jim Crow segregation or interpreting Gandhi's writings without knowledge of oppressive British rule.

Modern-day forms of domination include forms of servitude and bonded labor, contemporary forms of slavery and systems of oppressive government that suppress basic freedoms of speech, assembly, religion, and so on. For instance, an estimated twenty-seven million people worldwide are trapped in some form of economic bondage or slavery. According to International Justice Mission (IJM), "More children, women and men are held in slavery right now than over the course of the entire trans-Atlantic slave trade. Millions toil in bondage, their work and even their bodies the property of an owner. Trafficking in humans generates profits in excess of 12 billion dollars a year for those who, by force and deception, sell human lives into slavery and sexual bondage. Nearly 2 million children are exploited in the commercial sex industry."[20]

Discrimination and subordination are also a part of the daily existence of far too many people in the world today. Hundreds of millions of people must keep their religion and worship a secret because of intolerance or state sanction. In India, millions of Dalits, previously known as untouchables, are still treated as second-class citizens, relegated to the most menial jobs, and the targets of social isolation and discrimination.

Third is the root cause of violence. Both violence and the threat of violence often fuel injustice, as violence stifles hope and breeds resentment. Violence strips away any semblance of security and traps people in a straitjacket of fear. Violence can easily beget violence, turning into a vicious cycle that is difficult to slow down or stop. Dr. King captures this ethic when he said, "But we will never have peace in the world until men everywhere recognize that ends are not cut off from means, because the means represent the ideal in the making and the end in progress."[21]

Jesus teaches an alternative way rooted in peacemaking. Christ taught us to love our enemies and to turn the other cheek. Time and time again we fail to heed these instructions. Peacemaking requires getting in the way of violence and exposing the lies of its promised redemption. Jesus teaches us to break the cycle of revenge by loving our enemies and through the transformative power of forgiveness. Violence and the threat of violence take place in many vicious forms, from gang violence to domestic and sexual violence to the wanton violence associated with ethnic cleansing and genocide. According to the UN Development Fund for Women, one in five women is a victim of rape or attempted rape in her lifetime. The 2002 World Report on Violence and Health reports that violence kills more than 1-6 million people every year.

Last is the root cause of exclusion from community. Jesus made restoring the outcasts, the excluded, the Gentiles and the exiles to full community a central part of his ministry.[22] Jesus directly challenged the Pharisees' purity practices that separated people into the pure and the impure (Matthew 15:1-9). In the familiar parable of the Good Samaritan (Luke 10:29-37), Jesus confronted priests, Levites and anyone else who hated or excluded Samaritans or other ethnic groups from the circle of compassion.[23] Jesus' table fellowship with outcasts and the unclean challenged the central practice of purity at meals exercised by the Pharisees.

Time and time again, Jesus is seen healing and welcoming lepers, forgiving and embracing prostitutes, and breaking down false barriers that divide and alienate. Modern forms of exclusion include the interlocking "isms" of racism, classism, sexism and ageism—which perpetuate hierarchies of power and inequality. At the heart of the debate around immigration reform are issues surrounding exclusion and how we choose to treat the stranger among us. Instead of focusing on this issue, the debate has been polarized over stridently divergent definitions of justice. Proponents of immigration reform argue that justice requires granting an earned path to citizenship to an estimated thirteen million undocumented immigrants residing within the United States and discontinuing unjust deportations, harassment and discrimination. Opponents of citizenship also appeal to a justice argument, arguing that justice requires deporting people who have broken the law and are in the country illegally. However, deporting thirteen million people is both impractical and immoral in light of the biblical injunction to welcome the stranger among us. A broken immigration system negatively impacts us all, forcing many families to live in the shadows and in fear. While reform raises many difficult and complex issues around enforcement, rule of law and citizenship, we must shape the debate around biblical principles of compassion, mercy and inclusion.

ADDRESSING ROOT CAUSES RATHER THAN SIMPLY SYMPTOMS

Underneath every injustice and crisis are layers of root causes. These complexities can often be paralyzing and overwhelming. My wife has become obsessed with the proliferation of crime and detective shows that clutter prime-time television, including *CSI Miami* and *New York, NUMB3RS, Cold Case,* etc. While I'm far from an expert or avid watcher, I'm amazed by our culture's infatuation with crimes and solving mysteries. Most of the shows are adaptations of real-life cases, modified and often exaggerated for a television audience. In almost every show we see a crime take place, then a flashback that provides clues around the motives behind the crime and who the culprit may be. Apprehending the criminal requires careful questioning of witnesses and suspects, meticulous analysis of evidence and an often elaborate mapping out of the connection between seemingly disparate clues.

Transformed nonconformists must apply the same degree of rigor in mapping the injustices that we see in the world around us. We must understand the ways in which these four biblical forms of injustice interact with each other, often causing a chain reaction that exacerbates the original injustice. The crisis of HIV/AIDS provides a compelling and concrete illustration of this phenomenon.

I have a photograph that I keep posted on my desk as a constant reminder of the friends that I've lost and the communities that have been devastated due to the AIDS crisis. The photo was taken during the summer of 2000 in a rural village outside of Lusaka, Zambia. I spent a summer working with a development NGO called Africare around HIV prevention programs targeting young people. The photo shows an old man who is already a great grandfather, sitting with his back facing a group of his grandchildren who are staring expectantly in his direction. The epidemic had turned upside down expected social roles. In the sunset of his life, this elderly man must now serve as the caretaker for seven children, all orphaned by AIDS. In an era of life in which his children should be caring for him, this grandfather must now serve as the sole caretaker for his grandchildren because his children's lives were stolen by AIDS.

After a summer in Zambia listening to people's stories and witnessing firsthand the destruction caused by the epidemic, it became clear to me that just as the HIV virus attacks the weakest parts of a compromised immune system, AIDS disproportionately strikes the weakest members of our society. In 2000, most health clinics were only able to offer palliative care to ameliorate people's pain before they suffered an inexorable death. Prevention programs consisted largely of posting billboards warning about the deadly consequences of unprotected sex and telling young people to abstain. Yet these responses were grossly inadequate and failed to address an entire set of root causes that also had to be addressed in order to stem the tide of the disease.

The root causes examined earlier were all at play in the context of the epidemic, including unjust domination, unjust greed, unjust violence and unjust exclusion. Unjust domination was evident in women's lack of power to say no to sex in many countries and their inability to require their partners to use a condom. Many young girls contract the virus due to exploitative relationships with older men who promise to pay their school fees, give food or offer other trappings of a better life in exchange for sex. Unjust violence fuels the epidemic as rape is often used as a weapon of war and is alarmingly common in some of the most affected countries. Unjust exploitation came into play as greed fueled the exorbitant cost of AIDS drugs, which were almost entirely out of reach for most people living with HIV. In 2000 the average cost of a year's worth of life-prolonging AIDS medicine cost thirty times as much as the annual income of the average Zambian. These prices were driven higher due to excessive pharmaceutical profits and to companies' initial resistance to the production and distribution of generic drugs in resource-poor settings. People living with HIV also suffered from unjust exclusion. A shroud of silence, stigma and shame prevented people from getting tested and stigmatized people living with HIV. AIDS had become the leprosy of our time as social death often precedes a physical death.

These root causes form a web that has to be disentangled in order to reverse the epidemic. As a result of these interlocking injustices, the Student Global AIDS Campaign embraced a comprehensive approach to addressing the crisis, consisting of: combating sexual violence and gender inequality, advocating for cheaper AIDS drugs through reduced prices and greater access to generic drugs, connecting the fight against AIDS to the broader fight against poverty, and working to eradicate stigma and discrimination against people living with HIV.

When I try to see the HIV/AIDS crisis through God's eyes, the acronym Human Immunodeficiency Virus (HIV) takes on a dramatically different meaning and becomes an opportunity to "Heal the International Village." AIDS exposes our deepest fears and prejudices around issues of sex, sexuality, drug use and gender. Too many in the church have fallen back on negative moral judgment that either blames or closes the door to those most at risk. Some Christians still falsely believe that AIDS represents a punishment for sin, just as lepers were often blamed for their condition during the time of Christ. Fortunately, the majority of churches have moved from a posture of blame and condemnation to one of compassion and love. Stopping the AIDS epidemic requires nothing less than overcoming our fears around otherness and addressing the very root causes of people's vulnerability and marginalization. Who do I mean by the "other"? In ancient Israel the other would refer to the leper, the sex worker, the sick and the poor. In today's age of AIDS, the other is too often the IV drug user, the sex worker or the gay man or woman. But after spending a summer in Zambia, I was filled with the hopeful realization that God had given us the tools to fight HIV/AIDS and in the process heal a great deal of the world's brokenness. What was missing was the social and political will. Generating social and political will represents the job of transformed nonconformists.

Transformed nonconformists can apply the root causes of unjust domination, violence, exclusion and exploitation to better understand and overcome almost any injustice. We must take some invaluable cues from Jesus Christ, who modeled a commitment to expose and address injustice in his midst. But first we must get beyond many of the false and misleading aliases that obscure our understanding of Christ's countercultural and even revolutionary nature.

CHAPTER 3

FOLLOWING A HOLISTIC JESUS

WE DO CHRIST A DISSERVICE WHEN we deradicalize his ministry. Too often Jesus becomes a meek and mild Savior that had little or nothing to say to the religious and political powers of his time. This is a far cry from the Jesus portrayed in Scripture. In *The Politics of Jesus*, biblical scholar Obery Hendricks presents a convincing case as to why Jesus of Nazareth was a political revolutionary, arguing:

> Now to say that he [Jesus] was "political" doesn't mean that he sought to start yet another protest party in Galilee. Nor does it mean that he was "involved in politics" in the sense that we know it today, with its bargaining and compromises and power plays and partisanship. And it certainly doesn't mean that he wanted to wage war or overthrow the Roman Empire by force.
>
> To say that Jesus was a political revolutionary is to say that the message he proclaimed not only called for change in individual hearts but also demanded sweeping and comprehensive change in the political, social, and economic structures in his setting in life: colonized Israel. . . . It means that Jesus

sought not only to heal people's pain but also to inspire and empower people to remove the unjust social and political structures that too often were the cause of their pain.[1]

Hendricks contextualizes what it meant to be political and a revolutionary in the time of Christ. This context is critical, because Jesus is easily misunderstood when taken out of his political, economic and social context. In a 2007 workshop, Rev. Freddie Haynes reinforced this point, saying, "any time a text is taken out of its context it means you are being conned." In the seminal book *Jesus and the Disinherited*, Howard Thurman aptly describes Jesus' context in that Jesus of Nazareth was a poor Jew whose words "were directed to the House of Israel, a minority within the Greco-Roman world, smarting under the loss of status, freedom, and autonomy, haunted by the dream of the restoration of a lost glory and former greatness."[2] The Jews were still searching and waiting for a Messiah that would deliver them from Roman oppression and restore them to political, social and economic power. This explains why the Israelites could move so quickly from proclaiming Hosanna in the highest on Palm Sunday as Jesus rode into Jerusalem riding a donkey to plotting his death just days later.

Jesus was a political revolutionary not because he wanted to force the world into a new, rigid political or social paradigm but because he was so attuned to the kingdom of God that he was creatively maladjusted from the ways of the world. As transformed nonconformists, we can expect the same implications for our own lives. To say that Jesus was "political" is to invite a backlash, because in contemporary culture these words evoke a contradictory image of someone that is equivocating, self-serving, or trying to manipulate people and events to get what they want. Meanwhile, *revolutionary* often evokes a simplistic sort of exoticism, the kind that celebrates troublemakers. You may be smarting right now, wondering, how dare someone accuse Jesus of making trouble?

These terms can be redeemed by considering the degree to which Jesus turned the norms and expectations of his time upside down. Jesus was falsely accused of the political act of sedition and was killed by crucifixion, a death reserved for "trouble-makers" of the worst kind in ancient Rome. To be revolutionary in discipleship terms is to make an allegiance with heaven and kingdom values. This primary allegiance will inevitably rub up against the ways of the world. To be a revolutionary is to seek to transform minds and hearts toward a radical commitment to justice and love.

THE CHARTER OF A NEW ORDER

No single piece of Scripture summarizes the countercultural ethic of Jesus more than the Beatitudes that Jesus delivered during his Sermon on the Mount. The passage is like Jesus' Super Bowl sermon in which he lays out a bold and provocative vision, contrasting broken attitudes of the world with the redeemed attitudes of Christ. Jesus says:

> Blessed are the poor in spirit, for theirs is the kingdom of heaven. Blessed are those who mourn, for they will be comforted. Blessed are the meek, for they will inherit the earth. Blessed are those who hunger and thirst for righteousness, for they will be filled. Blessed are the merciful, for they will be shown mercy. Blessed are the pure in heart, for they will see God. Blessed are the peacemakers, for they will be called sons of God. Blessed are those who are persecuted because of righteousness, for theirs is the kingdom of heaven. Blessed are you when people insult you, persecute you and falsely say all kinds of evil against you because of me. Rejoice and be glad, because great is your reward in heaven, for in the same way they persecuted the prophets who were before you. (Matthew 5:1-12)

In the first three centuries of the church, this was the most referenced biblical passage.[3] For instance, when Justin Martyr wrote his First Apology in about A.D. 154, he quoted fully from the teachings of this sermon.[4] The sermon also represents the largest block of Jesus' teachings in the New Testament and served as the manual for teaching what it meant to be a Christian in the early church.[5]

As a declaration of the new kingdom of God, the Sermon describes the character, priorities, values and norms of the new age Jesus came to inaugurate. Each of the Beatitudes announces a blessing that comes with participation in the kingdom of God. Each of the main teachings in the Sermon is actually a pointer to the way of deliverance that we are given when the kingdom breaks into our midst.[6] For example, each Beatitude begins with the joy, happiness, blessedness and good news of participation in God's gracious deliverance. Each Beatitude ends by pointing to the reality of God's coming reign: in God's kingdom, those who mourn will be comforted, the humble will inherit the earth, those who hunger for righteousness will be filled, mercy will be shown, people will see God, peacemakers will be called children of God and the faithful will be members of the kingdom of God. These Beatitudes are echoed in Paul's letters and are deeply rooted in the whole Bible as the heart of biblical virtue. They picture what it means to be a follower of Jesus by capturing Jesus' own virtues.[7]

The Beatitudes contrast the world as it is with the world as is should be. Yet we often view the Beatitudes as ideals too high for us to reach up to or as lovely sentiments that are impossible for practical living.[8] The Beatitudes are not mere inner attitudes, vague intentions or moral convictions only; they are regular practices to be engaged in. The church is called to stand for the world as it should be; when it does not it risks abandoning its calling and mission.

So often the world recognizes and even rewards the exact opposite set of attitudes as the Beatitudes. Instead of "blessed are the meek," the cutthroat, hypercompetitive and arrogant often advance. Instead of "blessed are those who mourn," we are conditioned to be tough and not wear our emotions on our sleeves. "Blessed are those who thirst after righteousness" becomes "blessed are they that thirst after power at all costs," often rationalizing that the means will justify the ends. In our criminal justice system, "blessed are the merciful" is replaced by "blessed are the punitive." Instead of "blessed are the pure in heart," our politics and business culture too often bless the corrupt, disingenuous and duplicitous as long as they can get away with it.

The church is called to be on the cutting edge of modeling a new community and developing disciples who embody a countercultural set of attitudes in the world. In other words, we are called to create kingdom space here on earth, providing a foretaste of God's kingdom come through our actions and witness. Instead, we often become naturalized as citizens of the world rather than the kingdom of God. Just as the Jews felt pressured and coerced to adopt the attitudes and ways of Rome or Babylon, we are under immense pressure to adopt the dominant ways of the culture around us. If we aren't careful and conscientious, Babylonian or American values supplant and get counterfeited as Beatitude values.

GETTING IN THE WAY OF INJUSTICE

One of my favorite heroes of the civil rights movement still alive is Congressman John Lewis. Congressman Lewis served as the chair of the Student Nonviolent Coordinating Committee during crucial years of the civil rights struggle and led a brave band of marchers across the Edmund Pettus Bridge on what is now known infamously as "Bloody Sunday." I have heard Congressman Lewis speak on many occasions, most recently at the opening night of a three-day Mobilization to End Poverty in April 2009. Every time he speaks he repeats a favorite refrain calling on people to make a conscious decision to "get in the way" of injustice. "Getting in the way of injustice" requires making a conscious decision in the face of danger, and often requires great sacrifice.

Glen Stassen and David Gushee count forty times in the Synoptic Gospels (Matthew, Mark and Luke) when Jesus consciously decides to get in the way of injustice and confront the powers and authorities of his day.[9] In his initial sermon at Nazareth described in the fourth chapter of Luke, Jesus aligns himself with the long legacy of prophets who have come before him who also chose to "get in the way" of injustice. He reads from the prophet Isaiah proclaiming that "the spirit of the Lord is upon me, because he has anointed me to bring good news to the poor" (Luke 4:18 NRSV). Jesus proclaims that his ministry is inextricably linked to the struggles of the poor and to liberating the oppressed. Until recently I had glossed over Jesus' words after he closes the book and proclaims that these words have been fulfilled by his coming. Jesus goes on to criticize the Jews for their provincialism and xenophobia toward non-Jews. What appeared to be a proud and supportive congregation quickly turns into an angry mob that drives Jesus out of the temple and tries to throw him off a cliff. When the words of Jesus shake our sense of security and disrupt our notion of normalcy we often simply throw them out, deciding that they were meant to be taken metaphorically and not literally. I find this to be particularly true when it comes to the radical and provocative teachings, prescriptions and warnings that Jesus said about the ever uncomfortable topic of wealth and money.

Jesus' political party. Leading into each election, people often debate and speculate which political party Jesus would vote for and belong to if he were physically with us today. Both progressive and conservative Christians are guilty of this abuse. Due to the megaphone-like voice and disproportionate influence of the Religious Right during the 1980s and 1990s, Jesus was more often than not associated with voting Republican. Sojourners came out with a simple but provocative slogan prior to the 2004 election, saying, "God is not a Republican or a Democrat." In other words, Jesus does not fit neatly into an ideology or party platform. The question of Jesus' political preference is ironic given the degree to which Jesus rejected the overly restrictive political options of his own time. Why would his decision be different two-thousand-plus years after his death and resurrection? If Jesus were to become partisan, he would surely be partisan for the weak, the marginalized and the impoverished.

Jesus faced a series of concrete political options during his time. In Jewish culture there were several different worldviews that Jews developed to please God and respond to Roman oppression. Jesus could have joined the Saduccees or the Herodians, the Jewish religious officials drawn from the wealthy aristocracy who collaborated with the Roman rulers. This choice would have given him great access to power and influence over religious affairs. Instead, Jesus rejected their accommodation with Rome and was an outspoken critic of their hypocrisy. Jesus could have aligned himself with the Pharisees, religious leaders who practiced a strict code of piety, serving as arbiters of the requirements of Hebrew law. The Pharisees would have provided a natural fit for him as a practicing Jew and aspiring rabbi. Instead, Jesus rejected their intensification of the law's requirements even while he affirmed the values of love, forgiveness, etc., that were behind the law. Jesus could have pursued a monastic lifestyle by joining with the Essenes, who withdrew from mainstream society in the wilderness in order to live a more pure and highly ascetic existence. Yet Jesus refused to separate himself from society and instead chose to make the renewal of the people of God the primary focus of his ministry. Finally, Jesus could have joined the Zealots, who politically opposed Roman occupation and sought to overthrow the Roman Empire through revolutionary violence.[10] Instead, Jesus rejected violence (e.g., Mt 5:37-39; 26:52) while supporting the goal of liberation for all people through nonviolent means.[11]

Saduccees, Pharisees, Essenes and Zealots were so preoccupied by the political and cultural ideology of their day that they were unable to see or hear Jesus' proclamation of the kingdom of

God. They simply missed it. We risk repeating the same mistake based on the ways in which our understanding of Jesus gets clouded and distorted by our own social location and worldview. Jesus wasn't at home with any of the "parties" of his day, even though the earth is his and the fullness thereof, and even though he willfully came to abide among his own. Ultimately the great iconic image of Jesus recenters all political and theological imagination in the cross, outside the gates of religious power and on the receiving end of political power. From there he appears to be judged, but in reality he judges all and finds them wanting (Colossians 2:15). The cross becomes the ultimate symbol of subversive and revolutionary power. Jesus triumphs over death only after taking on humanity's inequity.

RECOVERING JESUS FROM IDENTITY FRAUD

After the 2004 presidential election, Jim Wallis raised the provocative question "How did Jesus come to be known as pro-rich, pro-war, and only pro-American?" It felt as though Jesus had been hijacked by an overly narrow agenda and distorted image. As Brian McLaren points out, Christians were searching for "'a new kind of Christian'—not an angry and reactionary fundamentalist, not a stuffy traditionalist, not a blasé nominalist, not a wishy-washy liberal, not a New Agey religious hipster, not a crusading religious imperialist, and not an overly enthused Bible-waving fanatic, but something fresh and authentic and challenging and adventurous."[12]

Groundbreaking survey data in the recent book *unChristian* reinforces the notion that Christianity is suffering from an acute and alarming public image problem. According to a 2006 survey, two out of every five (38 percent) young outsiders (non-Christians) claim to have a bad impression of present-day Christianity.[13] Eighty-five percent had a positive impression toward Christianity's role in society in 1996. In national surveys among young people, the three most common perceptions of present-day Christianity were anti-homosexual (91 percent), judgmental (87 percent) and hypocritical (85 percent).[14] The following negative perceptions are also embraced by the majority of young adults: old-fashioned, too involved in politics, out of touch with reality, insensitive to others, boring, not accepting of other faiths and confusing. These negative impressions of Christianity represent one of the greatest stumbling blocks to modern-day evangelism.

Greater civic and political engagement among Christians addressing the most pressing social justice issues of our time could serve as one of the best antidotes to turn around these negative impressions and stereotypes. Thus, embracing a transformed nonconformist faith will help to rebrand Christianity, saving the image of Christianity from itself. This may seem counterintuitive. If young nonbelievers are already complaining that Christians are too political, why would increased civic engagement rescue and redeem Christianity? Because Christians have been known over the past two decades primarily based on what we are against, particularly in terms of the focus of many Christians exclusively on social wedge issues. The Religious Right's foray into politics over the past thirty years has often given Christian political engagement a bad name, demonstrating the risks of aligning our agenda with one political party and focusing on only a narrow set of issues. Too many Christians and non-Christians alike feel burned and bruised by this model, which has precipitated a turn away from political and social engagement. As a result, Christians have been perceived as primarily engaged in divisive causes such as opposing abortion and gay marriage. While these hotly contested issues are very important, they come at very little direct cost to the lives and welfare of those advocating for change and often come at the expense of a range of issues central to the Bible such as fighting poverty, promoting peace and being good stewards of God's creation.

Through my travels and conversations with a broad spectrum of Christians, I have identified six ways in which people often misread or overly restrict Jesus' message and ministry.[15] I want to introduce you to the bling bling Jesus, the apocalyptic Jesus, the privatized Jesus, the Che Jesus, the apolitical Jesus and the Constantinian Jesus.

The *bling bling Jesus* has become one of the fastest growing and most pernicious distortions of Jesus, mirroring an increasingly hedonistic culture that glorifies the ostentatious lifestyles of the rich and famous. At worst, Jesus resembles a "playa" straight out of a music video wearing his gold chains and driving a Bentley. In this view, God becomes a heavenly ATM machine dispensing material blessings to reward those that tithe and are faithful.

While it is easy to write off the more egregious "name it and claim it" and "health and wealth" forms of this Jesus exemplified by the ministry of televangelists like Creflo Dollar and Benny Hinn, a bling bling or "prosperity gospel" has seeped into the theology of many churches and our spirituality in subtle but still harmful ways. Even more mainstream preachers like Joel Osteen argue that wealth represents the evidence of God's favor. One can extrapolate from this argument that the poor are poor either because of their own doing or because God has not shown them the same kind of favor. This is misleading and bad theology. God does want abundant life for everyone; however, Christ reserved some of his most scathing criticism against wealth that is not shared. Following a bling bling Jesus also leads to an overly transactional faith, in which we are constantly trying to get things from God rather than trying to live in God's will and experience blessings through our relationship with God. Through a bling bling Jesus, the focus of faith becomes misdirected toward seizing the crown rather than taking up the cross to follow Christ. Christ called on us to deny ourselves, take up our cross and follow him (see Matthew 16:24).

The *apocalyptic Jesus* is most associated with dispensationalist and fundamentalist theology, which often argues that since Jesus is coming back anyway, we don't have to worry about the health of our planet or the welfare of society. This Jesus was popularized through the record-breaking sales of the Left Behind series, sixteen bestselling novels by Tim LaHaye and Jerry Jenkins dealing with the end times. In this scenario famine, floods and conflict (particularly in the Middle East) become signs of the coming Armageddon. If the world is in decay and is heading toward destruction, there is little point in making the world a better place. This theology is often based on a misreading of the book of Revelation. John writes this letter using an apocalyptic genre of literature from the island of Patmos, addressing Christians in the seven churches on the mainland who are smarting under Roman persecution and occupation. The truth is that we don't know when Jesus will return. Two millennia have passed since many of the first Christians believed Christ would return within their lifetime. Instead of expending our energy speculating on the time of Christ's return, we should invest our time and talents in spreading the gospel and building God's kingdom here on earth. This is the true call of discipleship.

Subscribers to the *privatized Jesus* view a relationship with Christ as a private possession and the penultimate goal of Christianity. At worst, faith becomes reduced to fire insurance from hell. Followers of a privatized Jesus wholeheartedly support evangelism and proselytizing but ignore and often deny the social, economic and political implications of the gospel. Jim Wallis counters this overly narrow focus in *The Call to Conversion*, stating that "the goal of biblical conversion is not to save souls apart from history but to bring the kingdom of God into the world with explosive force; it begins with individuals but is for the sake of the world. . . . Our own salvation, which began with a personal decision about Jesus Christ, becomes intimately linked with the fulfillment of the kingdom of God."[16] Many churches in the Global South have better reconciled the false tension between evangelism and social justice through the concept of integral mission. Integral mission says, "If we ignore the world, we betray the word of God which sends us out to serve the world. If we ignore the word of God we have nothing to bring to the world. Justice and justification by faith, worship and political action, the spiritual and the material, personal change and structural change belong together."[17] I couldn't have said it better myself.

On the opposite extreme of the privatized Jesus is the *Che Jesus,* named after the iconic Cuban revolutionary figure Che Guevara. As someone who has been inspired by many strains of liberation theology, the Che Jesus has been a particularly enticing alias. Followers of the Che Jesus view Christ exclusively through the radical lens of liberation. Jesus' sole purpose becomes defending and emancipating the poor and marginalized. The need for a personal, redemptive relationship with Christ gets lost and overshadowed by an obsession with justice.

I have already made the case that justice represents a critical and indispensable focus of Jesus' message and ministry, but it should never be mistaken as the totality of his ministry. God wants an intimate and personal relationship with each and every one of us, and based on that relationship, God wants to enlist us in God's purposes in the world. Our vision of justice is rooted in God's kingdom, which can't be realized by human action alone. We must remember that because of Christ's victory on the cross, we have an eschatological hope that strengthens and empowers us in the midst of whatever existential challenges we might face. Even in the face of struggle and injustice, we know that ultimately we have the victory through Christ. A Che Jesus can also easily slip into an ideological mindset that equates Jesus' overriding concern for the weak and the vulnerable with the pursuit of a particular political or economic system. Jesus can't be reduced to simply an instrument to achieve some predetermined social and political vision or outcome.

Underneath many of our political debates are theological assumptions about Jesus' politics. One unspoken question is often whether Jesus was more of a socialist or a capitalist.[18] Christians can and will disagree on the best policies, programs and routes to achieve kingdomlike ends. However, we should be in agreement about the ends we seek to achieve. We must embrace Jesus' ends, which prioritize the needs of the least, the last and the lost. By this standard, the health of our politics and our economy should be measured around how the weak, the vulnerable and the marginalized are faring. This ultimate goal is never easy to achieve, but if it was truly embraced by all of the church, it could revolutionize our politics. We must either champion or oppose political and economic policies based on our best prudential judgment about whether they advance justice or further injustice.

A close cousin of the privatized Jesus is the *apolitical Jesus*. Christians who embrace the apolitical Jesus often believe in a public God but argue that the church is called to be the primary or exclusive instrument of God's righteousness and justice. Engaging in politics is viewed as corrupting and divisive. Politics represents the realm of compromise and deal-making while faith is the realm of the transcendent, the absolute and the pure. Thus, politics and faith become oil and water that should never mix. The separation of church and state often gets raised as an all-encompassing justification for disengagement from politics. Civic engagement and voting become an entirely personal enterprise.

I sympathize with this sentiment, particularly given the way religion has been so abused and misused to sanction a great deal of violence and oppression over the course of the church's history. Being ordained in the Baptist tradition, I'm a firm believer in the separation of church and state, which is practically sacrosanct in our tradition. However, if God is truly Lord over every aspect of our lives, then the political and economic realms are included as well. The National Association of Evangelicals document "For the

Health of the Nation" captures this belief when it says "We engage in public life because Jesus is Lord over every area of life. . . . To restrict our political concerns to matters that touch only the private and domestic spheres is to deny the all-encompassing Lordship of Jesus."[19] The separation of church and state does not require the segregation of faith from our public life. Our faith shapes a set of values that should undergird our approach to politics. As we will explore further, faith has also inspired and fueled many of the social movements that have transformed our nation and world.

The other problem with disengagement from politics is that our silence represents a form of participation. The great Mennonite theologian John Howard Yoder said it best: "It is possible to avoid having an outspoken political witness or to avoid criticizing existing structures, but then that silence is also a positive political action, accepting things as they are."[20] In other words, standing on the sidelines of a democratic political and electoral process gives implicit license to the people in power to carry out decisions in our name. Yoder also said, "To ask whether, as a people, we should be 'involved' is hardly ever the question. The question is on which side to be involved, which issues to give priority to, and what methods to use."[21] The question then is not whether to engage in politics but how to engage in ways that respect the separation of church and state and safeguard our independence and integrity.

Opposite the apolitical Jesus is the *Constantinian Jesus,* who has no problem combining faith with politics. Christians who identify with this Jesus repeat the same mistakes as the emperor Constantine, who sought to create a theocracy, fusing the church with the state. After having converted to Christianity in A.D. 313, Emperor Constantine issued an edict making Christianity the official religion of the empire. Constantine converted to Christianity partly out of political strategy and imperial expediency. He then used the cloak of Christianity to maintain his own power.[22] By doing so he tightly bound the survival of the empire with that of the church, and the church went from being a marginalized, disempowered group to occupying a central place in the corridors of power. In exchange, the church was forced to give religious license to the emperor, resulting in an "unholy alliance" between religious and political power. Constantine's incorporation of Christianity within the empire gave Christianity legitimacy and respectability, but it robbed it of its prophetic fervor. Engagement in contemporary politics presents many of the same temptations and risks. Becoming aligned with and overly dependent on one political party or leader often leads to being co-opted and used. Access to power can also be seductive, causing us to silence or tame our criticism because we don't want to lose that access. Yet access should never be an end in and of itself but instead represent a means to advance the cause of justice.

The holistic Jesus is the one who, contrary to the six false Jesuses so prominent in contemporary culture, leads us into responsible social action. While there are elements of truth in many of these six aliases, blindly following any one of them will lead you astray and block you from embracing a holistic Jesus, a Savior that calls on his disciples to advance evangelism and social justice, to seek both personal righteousness as well as communal righteousness, and to develop a personal, loving relationship with God and with neighbors and strangers alike. Following the holistic Jesus means learning from the dangers and excesses of the six false Jesuses and breaking out of the straightjacket of binary thinking, in which we feel compelled to make unnecessary black-and-white choices. We serve a God that can walk and chew gum at the same time.

From the privatized Jesus we can learn the critical importance of developing a personal relationship with Christ, which represents the jumping-off point for social action. From the apolitical Jesus, we can borrow a healthy precaution to never lose sight of our ultimate allegiance to God's kingdom when engaging in politics. From the prosperity Jesus, we can glean God's promise of a more abundant life. This won't conform to an ostentatious or hedonistic lifestyle but will ultimately be a more fulfilling life. From the Constantinian Jesus, we can draw a commitment to engage our culture and politics, seeking to transform both through values aligned with the kingdom. The apocalyptic Jesus reminds us that ultimately our fight is not against flesh and blood but against powers and principalities, thus we need God's strength and guidance in the midst of confronting injustice.

Following the holistic Jesus means embracing an active faith, a faith that is always on the move and is constantly making all things new. The holistic Jesus embodies the Beatitudes and refuses to get trapped in the narrow categories and confining labels of our culture. As disciples of a "holistic Jesus," a series of principles and parameters should guide our engagement in politics.

The Catholic Conference of Bishops released a document titled "Faithful Citizenship" leading up to the 2004 election. The booklet provides sound advice to guide Christian engagement in politics, instructing Christians to be "political but not partisan," "engaged but not used" and "principled but not ideological."[23] In other words, the church should never serve as a chaplain for any one party or a cheerleader for any candidate. We should be clear about our principles and priorities without impugning motives or engaging in name-calling. Following these principles will help us avoid the danger of becoming seduced by political power.

We can learn from the example of religious leaders within South Africa, who coined the term *critical engagement* to describe faithful engagement in politics. Following the African National Congress victory in 1994 and the election of Nelson Mandela as president, former anti-apartheid leaders had to develop a new form of political engagement. In the midst of their euphoria over Mandela's election, many church leaders foresaw the dangers of being co-opted by their friends in power and losing their ability to challenge the new government from a prophetic stance. Leaders developed the stance of critical engagement to balance newfound access while reserving and exercising the right to both praise and criticize government actions. Archbishop Desmund Tutu serves as a role model of this commitment due to his willingness to criticize former president Thabo Mbeki over his denial and negligent leadership around the AIDS crisis and his inability to pressure President Robert Mugabe to oppose blatant human rights abuses in Zimbabwe.

Following the holistic Jesus is never easy. We will stumble and make mistakes along the way. We will inevitably fall short and at times become blinded by one alias of Jesus over another. However, the holistic Jesus overcomes the best attempt to conceal him in false aliases. When our steps are most aligned with God's will, the holistic Jesus becomes most illuminated in our lives.

CHAPTER **4**

PRAGMATIC SOLIDARITY AND HOPEFUL ACTIVISM

I am sending you out like sheep among wolves. Therefore be as shrewd as snakes and as innocent as doves.

MATTHEW 10:16

If you have come to help me, you are wasting your time. But if you have come because your liberation is tied up with mine, then let us work together.

LILL WATSON, ABORIGINAL ACTIVIST

I DISTINCTLY REMEMBER AN EPIPHANY MOMENT that sharpened my understanding of the full definition behind the concept of solidarity. I had spent the year studying abroad in South Africa and had fallen in love with the resilience and beauty of the South African people. Based on my experiences, I vowed to relocate to South Africa once I finished my final year of college. Sizwe, the associate director of the School for International Training Programs in Cape Town, taught me the most about the rich culture of South Africa, particularly through the eyes of Xhosa tribal custom and history. During a three-day hike through the surreal landscape of towering mountains and crystal-blue sky in the Western Cape, Sizwe and I took a detour to conquer a peak and marvel at the brilliant sunset. I confided in Sizwe my plan to return to South Africa in order to continue the fight for social justice. I was afraid that the freedom movement in South Africa would dissipate in a fashion similar to the civil rights movement after major victories were achieved through the passage of the Civil Rights and Voting Rights Acts in 1964 and 1965. Sizwe responded with words that left an indelible mark on my mind and future. Very solemnly he said, "Adam, what you have shared is noble, but if you really want to help the people of South Africa, then you must return to America and stay there. Dedicate yourself to building enough influence in America so that you can work to change the policies of your wealthy and powerful country. This, my friend, will create a ripple effect that will be felt in South Africa. It would be selfish of you to return to South Africa and live full time." I have to admit that at first his words stung. Years later I would come to better understand the deep wisdom behind Sizwe's admonition. Sizwe helped me chart a course of solidarity, in which I carry the images of and relationships with people I've met around the world in my heart, mind and spirit. These people form a cloud of witnesses that speak into my decisions, and I sense them cheering me on as I try to try to advance the cause of social justice in the United States and around the world.

The solidarity dilemma is that it's far too easy to forget and feel distant from the people and experiences that motivate and necessitate our work for justice. The closer we get to the gravitational pull of power, the further away we often become from vulnerability and weakness. It is often not enough to intellectually know that we serve a God of justice. We must come to know the heart of God's love for justice through the stories and lives of real people. Being baptized in both people's pain and their triumph serves as an incredible source of inspiration and accountability. I realize that when I feel disconnected from the transforming power of relationships, I start to burn out.

The work of social justice is not simply about issues that must be addressed or policies that must be changed, but the real people, real families and real communities that lie behind all of the numbers and statistics. Sustaining creative maladjustment requires a regular dose of moral indignation and righteous anger, not in a destructive or life-negating form but in a life-affirming and kingdom-generating form. I believe that this need for human connection is why Gandhi traveled the incredible breadth of his native land of India by train after returning from a major victory over the British subordination of Indians in South Africa. Gandhi realized that he needed to reconnect with the people of India. Concrete and practical solidarity informs and sustains activism.

Without solidarity, activism risks becoming formulaic and numb to the realities faced by those whose backs are up against the wall and are experiencing an existential hell. Solidarity must be pragmatic because it is tied to a specific context and set of conditions or circumstances. Solidarity must also be intimate, tied to real relationships built on trust and accountability.

PRAGMATIC SOLIDARITY

I picked up the term and concept of "pragmatic solidarity" from Dr. Paul Farmer, who I've had the privilege of getting to know and work with, particularly in the context of activism around health and human rights issues. Dr. Farmer applies a radical Catholic faith and tenets of liberation theology to the field of medicine and public health. He adds into this already potent mixture the cultural sensitivities and listening disciplines of an anthropologist. According to Dr. Farmer, pragmatic solidarity is both "the desire to make common cause with those in need" and offering "goods and services that might diminish unjust hardship."[1] Making common cause with those in need is another way of describing the basis of solidarity, echoing a core tenet of liberation theology that God stands on the side of the oppressed and that Jesus exhibited a preference for the poor and marginalized. Solidarity requires being connected to the experiences and soliciting the views of the oppressed and incorporating these views into our observations, judgments and subsequent actions. Liberation theologians posit that we must listen to those most affected by an issue, form a judgment around the root causes behind an injustice, then act based on careful evaluation. This three-step process helps to inoculate activists from becoming overly heavy-handed and arrogant in their approach to addressing and solving problems. Dr. Farmer argues that a posture of penitence and indignation is critical to effective social justice work.[2] Penitence helps to disarm suspicion and build trust with people who have been oppressed, while indignation elicits great courage and passion.

Farmer cofounded Partners in Health (PIH), an organization that applies pragmatic solidarity to the crisis of public health facing the world's most impoverished and forgotten people. Through a number of trips to the Clinique Bon Sauveur, operated by PIH's partner NGO Zamni Lasante (ZL) in Cange, Haiti, I've witnessed pragmatic solidarity in action. Reaching Cange requires navigating across seemingly impenetrable roads that weave through central Haiti. After driving for over four hours across a distance that should only take one hour, you reach a hopeful oasis of modern medicine in the middle of an otherwise tumultuous sea of preventable disease and deprivation. The hospital overlooks an impoverished squatter community that was displaced by the construction of a hydroelectric dam. PIH has been carrying out HIV/AIDS prevention programs for over fifteen years in Cange, applying tenets of liberation theology to medicine by providing health care to the poor, regardless of their ability to pay. Despite criticism from many public health experts and conventional wisdom at the time, PIH/ZL launched the HIV Equity Initiative in 1998 to complement its prevention efforts by offering highly active antiretroviral (ARV) therapy free of charge to patients with advanced HIV. The program pioneered a model of directly observed therapy in which community health workers, called accompagnateurs, visit patients daily and supervise their pill taking while providing social and nutritional support. The success and publicity around this groundbreaking program became a model for the rest of the world, dispelling the myth and disproving the argument that providing treatment in a resource-poor setting would either be too costly or would lead to drug-resistant strains of the virus due to an assumed lack of adherence.[3]

My first trip to Cange was with a delegation of congressional staffers, NGO leaders and activists to investigate the impact of a $146 million Inter-American Development Bank loan to Haiti that had been blocked by the United States for political reasons. Our drive to Cange was blocked by a series of burning tires that had been thrown across the one road winding up toward the hospital. A strike over fuel prices obstructed our path forward. After a protracted negotiation with the protesters we were granted safe passage across the roadblock because we were transporting medicine that would save lives. On my second trip to Cange for an annual Health and Human Rights symposium, I participated in two days of community forums in which patients, doctors, community leaders and politicians discussed the intersection of health and human rights. I was humbled by the degree to which human rights took on more than simply an abstract or theoretical meaning. Instead, Haitians possessed an acute sense of their rights and eloquently championed the right to health as well as to security, jobs, education, and so on. PIH recognized that turning back the advance of HIV/

AIDS is inextricably linked to combating abject poverty, empowering women and improving overall public health. Through a human rights–centered approach, people living with HIV are not treated simply as patients that require diagnosis and treatment, but as children of God whose life chances have been circumscribed by disease and whose right to basic services has been callously denied.[4] Yet as much as the Clinique Bon Sauveur represented a lifesaving dam preventing a flood of premature death and unnecessary suffering in the central plateau of Haiti, the hospital's efforts were unable to transform the harsh realities of widespread underdevelopment and social injustice that have enveloped Haiti. Thus pragmatic solidarity required addressing the broken politics and external political interference that was also behind Haiti's duress as the poorest country in the Western Hemisphere. As a result, PIH has used its influence and credibility to challenge policies that are harmful to people's health. PIH formed a partnership with Physicians for Human Rights to mobilize health professionals and medical school students to advocate for major increases in U.S. funding for HIV/AIDS prevention and treatment programs.

The health of Haitians has been bruised and battered through successive waves of political violence and coups, economic exploitation and natural floods. The most recent catastrophic earthquake shocked the world and shined a spotlight on Haiti's plight. PIH has played an instrumental role in providing desperately needed medical care as practically the only health network left standing after the devastation of the earthquake. Thousands of the injured were treated both in Cange and in clinics supported by PIH across Haiti. Fortunately the global community has responded with unprecedented generosity and compassion. According to the *Chronicle of Philanthropy*, private U.S. donations a week after the earthquake reached $305 million, exceeding the $163 million raised the first week after the 2005 Indian Ocean tsunami.[5] It is easier to express solidarity when the images and stories of incredible tragedy blanket the news and airwaves. The challenge is to mobilize the same degree of urgency and response for the silent tragedies that take place every day just beneath the headlines, whether it's the millions of children that die prematurely every year due to malnutrition and vitamin A deficiency or the millions of innocent people that have been caught in the crossfire of armed conflicts in places like the Congo. The task of pragmatic solidarity is to shine a light on these crises and tragedies in order to awaken outrage and compassion. This requires reaching across the chasm of geography and distance to build relationships with people in need and learn how to amplify their struggle and tell their stories.

SNCC AND PRAGMATIC SOLIDARITY

The Student Nonviolent Coordinating Committee's (SNCC) heroic work during the freedom summer of 1964 represents another compelling example of pragmatic solidarity in action, following the three-step process of listening, judging and acting based on careful evaluation. As a sign of their pragmatic solidarity with black rural farmers, SNCC volunteers and organizers wore uniforms of denim, T-shirts and work boots.[6] By living among disenfranchised blacks in the South, they were able to build trust within these communities, listening to and learning from their stories. A process of discernment rooted in building deep relationships led SNCC leaders to conclude that voting rights represented the linchpin to securing civil rights and economic empowerment.

Based on this judgment, SNCC designed the Freedom Summer Project to shine a national spotlight on severe voting repression taking place across the South and to galvanize public opinion and political will behind voting-rights legislation. Through the Project, SNCC committed to starting twenty Freedom Schools, each staffed with fifteen teachers offering education in black history and culture, American social movements, and the arts. SNCC also developed thirty community centers across the state of Mississippi, assigning four volunteers in each of the eighty-two counties to coordinate voter registration.[7]

Bob Moses, the principal architect behind the project, epitomized the theology and praxis of pragmatic solidarity. Known as a philosopher, mystic and activist, Moses believed that an oppressed people, if affirmed in their created dignity through participation in a supportive community, could find power to voice their goals and to determine the steps necessary to realize them.[8] Moses embodied SNCC's incarnational commitment to work and live among disenfranchised and impoverished blacks in the South.

One of the often understated legacies of SNCC, and of the civil rights movement more broadly, is the degree to which faith served as a driving force awakening passion, sparking greater acts of sacrifice and sustaining the struggle. In the book *Building the Beloved Community*, Professor Charles Marsh documents the degree to which SNCC was motivated by "theological existentialism, holiness fervor, contemplative asceticism, social gospel idealism, Protestant liberal hope, and even some good old-fashioned other-wordliness."[9] SNCC sought to become "the enfleshened church," displaying a remarkable capacity to anchor itself in particular neighborhoods and accommodate its disciplines to local needs.[10] For example, the Founding Statement of SNCC positions a faith-inspired commitment to nonviolence as both an overriding ethic and a core tenet, stating that "nonviolence, as it grows from the Judeo-Christian tradition, seeks a social order of justice permeated by love. . . . Through nonviolence, courage displaces fear. Love transcends hate. Acceptance dissipates prejudice; hope ends despair. Faith reconciles doubt. Peace dominates war. Mutual regards cancel enmity. Justice for all overthrows injustice. The redemptive community supersedes immoral social systems. By appealing to conscience and standing on the moral nature of human existence, nonviolence nurtures the atmosphere in which recon-

ciliation and justice become actual possibilities."[11] Nonviolence
served as the glue that bound SNCC's vision and methodology of
organizing together. As a commitment to nonviolence ebbed within
the leadership of the organization, a fierce hope anchored in faith
was replaced by diffuse and unharnessed anger.

Marsh argues that the demise and dissolution of SNCC was
precipitated in large part by the replacement of the Christian
ethic of nonviolence, steadfast love and justice with a more secular and militant ideology of black power. This shift came to a
head in the 1966 victory of Stokely Carmichael over John Lewis
as the head of SNCC. In 1967 a new policy was passed to exclude
all white members from SNCC's ranks. SNCC subsequently re-
solved to become a "Third World Coalition of revolutionaries
who were anticapitalist, antiimperialist, and antiracist."[12] While
other historical and political factors also explained SNCC's demise, the loss of a faith-inspired hope played a pivotal role. Instead of working to redeem America, SNCC increasingly took on
a posture that the United States was malevolent and beyond redemption. SNCC's goals shifted from identifying social and economic ills that could be improved upon through organizing and
social reform to more elusive goals such as "ending racism in
America" and "developing black consciousness." These global
ambitions became disconnected from commitments to local organizing, and generated strategic confusion.[13] Removed from its
home in the church and local communities, the goal of building
the beloved community withered and died. Former chair and
Congressman John Lewis pointed out that black power shirked
the discipline and the focus that the commitment to nonviolence
engendered and sustained.[14] A faith commitment reminiscent of
the early SNCC is needed to guide and sustain activism among a
new generation of young leaders today, rooted in hopeful activism. In the face of both old and new injustices, solidarity must be
fueled by the power of hope.

HOPEFUL ACTIVISM

Activism without hope is like a balloon drained of air; it quickly deflates and loses its ability to rise in the air. Hope is the oxygen that inspires and sustains activism. Too often campaigns fail because of a deficit of hope. Too much spite, anger or malice suffocates the hope out of activism. Hope animates our vision of what's possible and guides what we are striving to achieve in the context of transformed nonconformism. Fortunately, hope is at the very heart of faith. Hope stems from an understanding of eschatology and soteriology. Soteriology is simply a theological term that connotes how we approach and understand salvation. Christ's death on the cross and resurrection gives us ultimate victory over death and injustice. Eschatology is how we approach the end times or death. The in-breaking of God's kingdom come began with Christ and will be fulfilled with his return. We should be reminded of this reality every time we say the Lord's Prayer.

Too often we can gloss over the power and full meaning behind the Lord's Prayer. The prayer often becomes overly diluted and formulaic as something we memorize and rehearse at the appropriate moments in a worship service. Yet during the time of Christ, the Lord's Prayer took on a more radical and subversive nature. For followers of Jesus to say "our Father, who art in heaven, hallowed be thy name" was to declare allegiance to God instead of to Caesar Augustus and Rome. The next familiar words, "thy kingdom come, thy will be done," place a commitment to God's kingdom above any other worldly kingdoms, whether it's the Roman Empire or systems of government today. In ancient Israel saying these successive statements publicly would mean committing the same crime of sedition for which Jesus was convicted and crucified.[15]

Brian Swarts[16] echoes the importance of the Lord's Prayer in shaping his public activism, saying "thy will be done, on earth as it is in heaven" is a prayer of justice; "it tells me that following God means living not according to the broken ways of the world, but with the compassion, justice and mercy of God." Acting on this prayer involves a countercultural commitment to the work of kingdom-building. I love the metaphor of kingdom-building because it is so all-encompassing. There is no aspect of life that escapes God's kingdom. The keys to God's kingdom are rooted in hope.

The German theologian Jürgen Moltmann encapsulates the profound power of hope in his book *Theology of Hope*. According to Moltmann, hope creates in a believer a "passion for the possible."[17] Moltmann writes, "Christianity is eschatology, is hope, forward looking and forward moving, and therefore also revolutionizing and transforming the present." In other words, because Christ inaugurated the inbreaking of the kingdom, our constant strivings to create a better world are aligned with God's purposes. Moltmann continues, "Faith binds man to Christ. Hope sets this faith open to the comprehensive future of Christ. Hope is therefore the 'inseparable companion' of faith." Yes, hope and faith are thus inextricably linked and mutually reinforcing.

Moltmann argues that the weakness of our faith must be sustained and nourished by patient hope and expectation, lest it fail and grow faint. He concludes that "without faith's knowledge of Christ, hope becomes a utopia and remains hanging in the air. But without hope, faith falls to pieces, becomes a fainthearted and ultimately a dead faith. It is through faith that man finds the path of true life, but it is only hope that keeps him on that path. Thus it is that faith in Christ gives hope its assurance."[18]

In *Jesus and the Disinherited*, Howard Thurman also captures the indispensable power of hope. Thurman writes, "[Christ] recognized fully that out of the heart are the issues of life and that no external force, however great and overwhelming, can at long last destroy a people if it does not first win victory of the spirit against them. . . . [Jesus] announced the good news that fear, hypocrisy, and hatred, the three hounds of hell that track the trail of the disinherited, need have no dominion over them."[19] Hope is the antidote to fear. Hope enables people to withstand incredible adversity and hold on even in the midst of persecution or seemingly impossible odds. Hope fuels and shapes our vision of a preferred future. For campaigns to be successful, they must harness and sustain hope. The fight against HIV/AIDS in South Africa demonstrates the indispensable role of pragmatic solidarity and hope in fueling social and political change.

WHAT HAPPENS TO A DREAM DEFERRED?

In 1998, a thirty-six-year-old South African woman named Gugu Dlamini disclosed on radio and television that she was HIV positive. Three weeks after speaking out, Dlamini was knifed to death by a group of her neighbors, many of which were rumored to be her ex-boyfriends.[20] The brutal killing became a stark wake-up call for people living with HIV in South Africa and resulted in the formation of the Treatment Action Campaign (TAC). In 1998, three million South Africans had already contracted the HIV virus, yet fewer than a hundred had spoken out openly about their disease. In both 2001 and 2005, I had the privilege of spending time with leaders of TAC. The campaign was founded in order "to ensure that every person living with HIV has access to quality, comprehensive prevention and treatment services to live a healthy life."[21]

TAC has mobilized the most effective social movement since the freedom struggle that overturned apartheid. The organization has mobilized thousands of people living with HIV and given them a platform to affirm their dignity and demand their rights. The campaign has remixed many of the anti-apartheid movement songs as a way to claim the AIDS struggle as a continuation of the freedom struggle. As of 2008, with more than sixteen thousand members, 267 branches and 72 full-time staff members, TAC has become the leading civil society force fighting for comprehensive health-care services for people living with HIV and AIDS in South Africa. Since 1998, TAC has held the South African government accountable for health-care-service delivery; campaigned against the denialism of the South African government; challenged the world's leading pharmaceutical companies to make treatment more affordable; and cultivated community leadership on HIV/AIDS. Their efforts have resulted in many life-saving interventions, including the implementation of a countrywide mother-to-child transmission prevention program and a countrywide antiretroviral treatment program, which required overcoming the intransigence of the South African government.

TAC has been effective in overcoming so much of the hopelessness that surrounds the AIDS crisis in South Africa by giving people living with HIV the will to live with dignity and by transforming the disease from a death sentence into a manageable disease. For years during the height of the AIDS struggle, Zachi Achmat, TAC's founder, refused to accept antiretroviral treatment until all South Africans were granted access. Zachi recalled an apocryphal tale about Christian X, the Danish king who began wearing the star of David after the Nazis invaded Denmark in 1940. The king's action prompted Christians throughout Denmark to do the same so that Jews would be indistinguishable from the rest of Danish society. TAC applied this Danish lesson of showing visible solidarity with those who are shunned and persecuted because of HIV/AIDS by producing what have now become iconic T-shirts with the simple phrase "HIV Positive" emblazoned on the front.

I distinctly remember returning from a trip to South Africa and rather absentmindedly wearing one of these famous TAC "HIV Positive" T-shirts into my Bally's gym. Upon entering the gym I started noticing a series of shocked and disapproving stares from other people working out. It took me a while to realize that people were reacting to my T-shirt. Even in a country in which HIV has become a manageable disease for so many people and is more socially accepted, wearing the T-shirt still represented a brazen act. The T-shirt demonstrates the beauty and essence of pragmatic solidarity, which echoes the apostle Paul's comparison of the church to a human body in 1 Corinthians. Whether you are living with HIV or not, wearing the T-shirt sends a provocative and transformative message that if one person is infected with HIV, then we are all directly affected; it represented a small but bold act of pragmatic solidarity.

In order to effectively combat the AIDS epidemic, TAC had to reawaken the power of hope in people's lives. Many people living with HIV across the world suffer a social death that precedes their physical death from AIDS, which serves as a powerful force in driving the disease underground, undermining prevention efforts and deterring people from getting tested. TAC started anonymous clubs for people living with HIV to teach treatment literacy and help people better manage their disease. These clubs created bonds of support, encouragement, fellowship and empowerment for people living with HIV, helping them learn to love themselves again and overcome the shame and fear so often associated with infection.

Through my work with youth HIV prevention in Zambia during the summer of 2000, I realized that prevention programs would ultimately fail without unlocking the power of hope. Without access to life-prolonging treatment, the disease remained a death sentence, leaving people with little to no incentive of getting tested. Access to treatment had the power of unleashing hope and changing public perception around the disease. Young people who lacked hope for their future made more risky and self-destructive decisions. The risk associated with a disease that isn't fatal for another five to ten years after infection is less urgent than meeting more basic and pressing needs like access to food. Hope is critical to changing behavior, giving people more to live for and a greater will to take more precautions to protect their health and the health of others.

THE JUBILEE 2000 CAMPAIGN

A number of occupational hazards complicate living out pragmatic solidarity. One danger in advocacy is that, as an organization or campaign gets too close to power, it can quietly compromise its goals or lose touch with the very people most affected by the injustice. In the process, conflicts can arise between the people directly affected by an injustice and those who have pledged to advocate on their behalf. The Jubilee campaign to cancel "third world" debt provides an excellent illustration of these challenges. I have had the honor of being intimately involved in the Jubilee campaign in the United States since 1997.

I distinctly remember the first time I heard about the modern-day debt crisis. Marie Dennis of the Maryknoll Catholic sisters gave a mesmerizing presentation at the 1999 Call to Renewal Conference in Washington, D.C., in which she painted a vivid picture of countries across sub-Saharan Africa, Latin America and Asia being caught in a debt trap, paying more to service their debts than they received in new aid each year. My moral sensibilities were shaken by this hypocrisy and irony. I felt as though scales were falling from my eyes as I listened to the pernicious effects of the debt crisis, which was forcing countries into a rat race of unsustainable debt repayments and exacerbating unnecessary human suffering.

The Jubilee 2000 campaign represents one of the few truly global campaigns for economic justice. While people from across the developing world had been crying out for years for debt cancellation, the campaign gained momentum first in the United Kingdom then in the United States in the mid 1990s. The Catholic and Protestant churches played a pivotal role, applying an obscure text in Leviticus calling for the periodic cancellation of debt in order to right relationships to the modern-day crisis of debt. Appealing to the Jubilee Year lent greater urgency and provided a moral imperative behind the campaign. The origins of the debt crisis were tied to the geopolitics surrounding the Cold War, in which many countries were given lavish loans with very little accountability by wealthy countries and multilateral banks. To make matters worse, there is no system of bankruptcy or amnesty for countries within the international economy that can't repay their loans. Sadly, in most cases the monies from these loans were never used for the original purpose of fighting poverty and advancing economic development. Instead, the loans and aid enriched many corrupt and dictatorial regimes that pledged loyalty to the United States in the chess game of the Cold War struggle. One of the most heartbreaking and egregious examples is loans that were given to South Africa in the 1970s and '80s, which were used to maintain the system of apartheid. Another pernicious example is loans given to former President Mobutu Sesse Seko of the former Zaire, who brutally oppressed his people and siphoned off money into a number of Swiss bank accounts. Despite the misuse of these loans by many governments, the countries are still forced to repay.

Tension filled the air like a fog during a meeting in Edinburgh at the 2005 G8 Summit. Leaders from Jubilee campaigns across the world were talking past each other as they described the painful and heartbreaking consequences of the debt crisis. The chasm between "developed" and "developing" countries was palpable and had to be traversed in order to maintain unity within the Jubilee movement. Leaders representing campaigns in the Global South made impassioned pleas to their allies in the North to shift their rhetoric and focus from championing "debt forgiveness" to supporting the repudiation of largely illegitimate and odious debts. The mantra "don't owe, won't pay" became their rallying cry. Jubilee South argued that the majority of the debts were illegitimate in the first place and must therefore be canceled if not repudiated. Many northern campaigns took a more pragmatic route, arguing that governments and international banks were unlikely to write off the debt but would forgive portions of the debt as long as safeguards were put in place to ensure the money was used for poverty-reducing programs. Leaders from the South had also grown exasperated with the taxing conditions and onerous timetables put in place by the World Bank and the IMF by which countries had to adhere in order to qualify for partial debt relief. The process, called the Heavily Indebted Poor Country Initiative (HIPC), forced countries to jump through a series of hoops that often took multiple years and made them further beholden to a series of often detrimental economic policies.

I joined the Steering Committee of the Jubilee USA Network in 2001, eventually becoming the co-chair in 2004-2005. The network was formed to coordinate and catalyze the actions of a broad cross-section of organizations committed to advancing debt cancellation, including faith groups, environmental, labor and human rights organizations. One of the challenges of working across a global context was the issue of accountability. For example, how should campaigns based in creditor or wealthy nations be accountable to the voices and perspectives of campaign leaders from heavily indebted countries? Whose voices should northern campaigns listen to when there were conflicting opinions among civil society leaders in heavily indebted countries?

In 2000 the Jubilee campaign was successful in convincing both President Clinton and President Bush to cancel 100 percent of the bilateral debt owed by many developing countries to the United States, in part by building a broad bipartisan coalition in Congress behind the cause of debt cancellation. The campaign then shifted gears to focus on the debt owed by over sixty countries to multilateral creditors, including the World Bank, International Monetary Fund, African Development Bank and the Inter-American Development Bank. Leading into the 2005 G8 Summit, the campaign worked to pressure and persuade leaders of the world's wealthiest countries (who wielded a controlling interest in both the World Bank and the IMF) to accelerate 100 percent debt cancellation for these heavily indebted countries.

Despite sometimes contentious differences in perspective, good lines of communication and relationships built up over time enabled campaigns in the Jubilee South to place a great deal of trust in the prudential judgment of the U.S. campaign to determine the best advocacy strategy for advancing debt cancellation in the U.S. political context. These bonds of pragmatic solidarity enabled the global campaign to remain intact and garner greater international legitimacy. Too often campaigns driven by NGOs in wealthy countries possess all the best intentions but end up re-creating and reinforcing the global power imbalances they seek to rectify by singlehandedly determining what's in the best interest of other countries. This hubris becomes justified by the rationalization that only they know what will work.

Campaigns must strike a very delicate and difficult balance between advocating for the ideal and advocating for what is deemed politically possible. Incremental victories are often critical for advancing a campaign and giving people a sense of their own power as long as the incremental approach does not lead to premature compromise. In the context of the Jubilee campaign, a pivotal but incomplete victory at the G8 Summit in 2005 secured 100 percent debt cancellation for eighteen countries. While an additional sixty-plus countries are in desperate need of cancellation, the victory established a precedent for 100 percent cancellation that could be built upon in the future. These critical decisions come down to strategy and tactics, which is the very character of a campaign.

CHAPTER 5
THE CHARACTER OF TRANSFORMED NONCONFORMISM

Then Saul dressed David in his own tunic. He put a coat of armor on him and a bronze helmet on his head. David fastened on his sword over the tunic and tried walking around, because he was not used to them.

"I cannot go in these," he said to Saul, "because I am not used to them." So he took them off. Then he took his staff in his hand, chose five smooth stones from the stream, put them in the pouch of his shepherd's bag and, with his sling in his hand, approached the Philistine.

1 SAMUEL 17:38-40

CREATIVE MALADJUSTMENT REQUIRES A series of organizing and advocacy skills and strategies to be effective, which are combined in a toolbox called campaigns. An entire book is needed to do justice to this topic alone. And in fact a number of manuals and how-to guides have been written, yet these guides often fall short in centering and contextualizing the nuts and bolts of organizing in a faith context or perspective. Ultimately, faith-based campaigns must seek to convert the hearts and minds of people and transcend an assessment of simply appealing to people's self-interest. Faith-inspired organizing taps into a shared story and motivation rooted in the transformative power of the Spirit.

The Bible reminds us that when there is no vision, the people perish (Proverbs 29:18). In the context of designing a campaign, where there lacks clear organization, the vision will perish. Dennis Jacobson says it best: "Vision without organization is fanciful. Organization without vision is moribund. To become realized, vision must be organized. To remain dynamic, an organization must be visionary."[1] Particularly in the faith context, we tend to be great on vision but weak on practical implementation. For instance, a campaign to achieve world peace or to end poverty may sound good and inspiring in its aims but will quickly stumble and fall because it isn't measurable, specific or achievable. In contrast, a campaign designed to pass a ballot initiative to increase the minimum wage as a step toward ending poverty still appeals to the long-term vision but is specific and achievable.

Thanks to my studies with Marshall Ganz, the story of David and Goliath has become my framework for understanding the power of organizing. Ganz helped me to see that this familiar story is about much more than the underdog defying the odds. David teaches us a lesson about the power of seeing obstacles through God's anointed vantage point. As you probably recall, the Israelites face the mighty Philistine Goliath in battle. Goliath taunts them, mocks God and intimidates them with his sheer size and strength. The Israelites are paralyzed and immobilized by their fear. No one among the Israelites has the courage to confront the mighty Philistine. In the place of Goliath, we can imagine whatever has bullied or taunted us during our lives. Social injustice

often takes on the persona and traits of Goliath, seeming overwhelming and intractable.

David, only a young shepherd boy at the time, agrees to face
Goliath. First King Saul hands David a sword and a body of armor.
Picture this scrawny shepherd boy weighed down by oversized armor and a sword. David sizes up Goliath and realizes that he can
never defeat him with these conventional weapons. Instead, he
must play to his strengths and exploit Goliath's greatest weakness.
David remembers all of the dangers that God has brought him
through, like when he defeated a lion that threatened his flock
with a single stone and a sling-shot.

David reconfigures the battlefield according to the unique gifts
that God has given him and steps out on faith to confront Goliath
with his sling-shot and five smooth stones that he finds in a brook
nearby. The rest is biblical history: David slays Goliath with a single stone, hitting the giant on the forehead. In the context of social
and political change, we too must identify both the strengths and
the weaknesses of the people whose minds and hearts we seek to
change. We must also learn to reconfigure the battlefield according to the gifts that God has given us.

Campaigns represent the means through which we reconfigure
the battlefield against injustice. Campaigns are highly energized, intensely focused streams of activity with specific goals and dead-
lines.[2] Campaigns that are ill-conceived, overly ambitious or poorly
executed often lead to burnout and will disillusion newcomers to
activism. Many campaigns also fail because the goals are too broad
and vague in scope. Successful campaigns possess three characteris-
tics: they make your organization stronger by giving people a sense
of their own power; they win concrete improvements in people's
lives; and over time they alter the relations of power, making leaders
more responsive to your concerns and interests in the future.[3]

Campaigns have both a rhythm and a deliberateness about
them. In his famous "Letter from a Birmingham Jail," Dr. Martin

Luther King lays out four steps for any nonviolent campaign: collection of the facts to determine whether injustices are alive, negotiation, self-purification and direct action. These echo Gandhi's three stages of persuasion, sacrifice and noncooperation. Effective campaigns have a way of escalating tactics over time in order to build greater pressure and apply increased leverage upon a decision-maker. Some of the key steps of any campaign include identifying who has the power to give you what you want, evaluating the human and financial resources that are needed, recruiting and enlisting allies, generating a better understanding of opponents and their interests, and determining what tactics will best achieve your goal.[4]

Campaigns require a combination of relational, motivational and strategic skills.[5]

Relationships form the lifeblood of effective campaigns. People are inspired to act and are often willing to make sacrifices in part because of their connections to other people. Motivational skills are developed through the power of public narrative that we explored in chapter one. Strategy is how we turn what we have into what we need to get what we want. Good strategy, like good jazz, is an ongoing creative process of learning to achieve a desired outcome by interacting with others to adapt to constantly changing circumstances.[6] Strategy is an interactive process of experimentation, learning and adaptation. Leaders experiment with different tactics, then learn to adapt based on a careful evaluation of their effectiveness in achieving a desired result. Campaigns often fail because they don't candidly and honestly evaluate the effectiveness of their action plan and make course corrections based on what is learned. According to Ganz, "the likelihood that a leadership team will devise effective strategy depends on the depth of its motivation, the breadth of its salient knowledge, and the robustness of its reflective practice."[7]

Effective campaigns also require building effective coalitions of

leaders and organizations, which often requires moving outside
our comfort zones. The media and political officials are often in-
trigued and impressed when unusual allies and strange bedfellows
come together around a shared issue or cause. One great example
of this was the Rolling to Overcome Poverty bus tour stop in Chicago prior to the 2004 election. At the time, Christa Mazzone
Palmberg was serving as the national organizer for Call to Renewal.
Christa reached out to churches from across the theological spectrum to solicit their support in planning and hosting an ecumenical service focused on overcoming poverty. A deep commitment to
theological diversity and bridge-building resulted in the most theologically diverse gathering in Chicago's recent history; a shared
commitment to fighting poverty served as the unifying glue holding the event together. Participants were able to put on hold many
other theological and political disagreements for the greater cause
of addressing poverty. This reflected the very ethos of Call to Renewal, which represented a broad table of faith-based organizations and denominational leaders united around the biblical imperative to overcome poverty.

Our strategy and tactics must also be consistent with our values. According to Dr. King, "in the final analysis, means and ends
must cohere because the end is preexistent in the means, and ultimately destructive means cannot bring about constructive ends."[8]
While some more aggressive and adversarial tactics may result in a
short-term victory, they can also burn bridges with the people you
are trying to influence. Striking the right balance of tactics is an art
and not a science. Tactics that alienate and offend the very people
you are trying to reach and enlist to support your cause are counterproductive. While these tactics may grab headlines, they often
lack the transformative power to change hearts and minds. At the
same time, campaigns of creative maladjustment will often spark
controversy, elicit criticism, or lead to either subtle or overt persecution. For example, Dr. King was criticized by many of his fellow

ministers for leading a bus boycott that caused such disruption and damage to business in Montgomery.

A generational disconnect exists around tactics used during previous movements. Sit-ins, large-scale civil disobedience and freedom rides have largely gone out of style and no longer seem relevant to our contemporary landscape. While there will always be a time and place to reinvent and apply these tactics, organizing today must be updated with the times to truly engage a new generation of transformed nonconformists. As difficult as it may be for a holdover like me to admit, we must better harness the power of technology. For example, social networking sites like Facebook and MySpace have become critical platforms for reaching and mobilizing young people. However, these platforms are not a substitute for the deeply relational nature of effective organizing. MoveOn represents the quintessential example of an organization that has grown exponentially by harnessing viral Internet growth. Whether or not you agree with their politics, the organization has pioneered the use of the Internet to build a virtual constituency of progressive activists who are being mobilized to participate in house parties, demonstrations and fundraising campaigns to raise money for ad campaigns.

The Internet has allowed people to connect and mobilize like never before. A great example is demonstrated through a close friend and former classmate of mine, Ricken Patel, who launched Avaaz, a global online network of activists promoting stronger protections for the environment, greater respect for human rights, and concerted efforts to end poverty, corruption and war. Avaaz.org seeks to close the gap between the world we have and the world most people everywhere want. Avaaz builds on the rise of a new model of Internet-driven, people-powered politics, which is changing countries from Australia to the Philippines to the United States. The core of their organizing model is their email list, operated in thirteen languages. By signing up to receive alerts, people are rapidly notified of urgent global issues and opportunities to achieve change. Avaaz members respond by rapidly combining the small amounts of time or money they can give into a powerful collective force. In just hours or days they can generate hundreds of thousands of messages to political leaders telling them to save a crucial summit on climate change,[9] hold hundreds of rallies across the world calling for action to prevent a genocide, or raise hundreds of thousands of euros, dollars and yen to support nonviolent protest in Burma.[10] In less than three years, they've grown to over 3.5 million members and have begun to make a real impact on global politics.[11]

Our best lessons in designing and leading campaigns often come through failure. During my first year as a graduate student at the Kennedy School, I was elected president of the Harvard-wide chapter of the NAACP. My executive team and I wanted to leverage the notoriety of the Harvard name in order to make a significant impact on federal education policy. While the NAACP had served as a tireless and consistent advocate and guardian of civil rights, the organization was struggling to figure out how to broaden a traditional civil rights agenda to include economic justice and reach a younger generation. Through our experiences volunteering in a struggling inner-city high school in Boston, our team came to the conclusion that unequal and inferior access to a quality education represented the greatest civil rights issue of our time. In response, we designed a bold national campaign called Rallying for Equity and Access to College and Higher Education (REACH), which sought to mobilize NAACP college chapters countrywide around the goal of educational equity. The campaign was designed to culminate in a national march with thousands of students on the Washington Mall to elevate educational equity to the top of the nation's political agenda. The campaign was heavy on vision but very weak on concrete, achievable goals. While we were able to sell the idea at the conceptual level to NAACP leadership, we were never able to get true buy-in or commitment from the national organization to invest real resources in the initiative due to the campaign's overly ambiguous goals and lack of a clear implementation plan. The campaign's demise was a sobering lesson in the importance of setting realistic goals tied to an effective strategy.

OVERCOMING THE GOLIATH WITHIN

I used to bemoan the fact that I wasn't alive during the 1950s or '60s, when injustice seemed so much more overt and movements seemed so much more robust. At that time there was no way to ignore the suffocating discrimination of Jim Crow segregation in the South. The task of realizing justice in our contemporary context often seems more difficult because injustice and inequality have become mutated genes that seem more invisible. The Goliaths of economic injustice and inequality may be more covert and institutionalized but are still pernicious. Goliaths are still embedded in systems and structures that subjugate and oppress.

In the face of modern-day Goliaths such as poverty, human trafficking and global climate change, we often become gripped by inertia, fear, self-doubt, impotence, isolation and even apathy.[12] These emotions become internalized and calcify into inaction. These Goliaths strip away our sense of agency, destroy our confidence and demoralize our spirits. They make us question that real change can ever take place, deceiving us into believing that we are too small or too weak and that the odds are just too great, that we aren't worthy of greatness. At his inauguration as president of South Africa, Nelson Mandela quoted a poem that challenges those internal Goliaths:

> Our deepest fear is not that we are inadequate. Our deepest fear is that we are powerful beyond measure. It is our light, not our darkness, that most frightens us. We ask ourselves, who am I to be brilliant, gorgeous, talented and fabulous?

Actually, who are you not to be? You are a child of God. Your playing small doesn't serve the world. As we let our own light shine, we unconsciously give other people permission to do the same. As we are liberated from our own fear, our presence automatically liberates others.[13]

In other words, God made us for a profound purpose. When we sit on our gifts or make a litany of excuses for why we aren't prepared or able, we block the manifest glory of God that is within us. Trying to tackle injustice based on our own limited abilities means playing small. Instead we must tap into the renewing power of faith to overcome the barriers that get in the way of transformed nonconformism.

The first and most common barrier is inertia.[14] Particularly in this Internet age, we are barraged and inundated with constant information and marketing campaigns enticing us to do or buy something. This information overload makes it more difficult to grab people's attention and solicit their commitment. After a while, we either start shutting out this information overload or become increasingly jaded about solicitations for our time and attention. Inertia becomes our fallback and the keeper of the status quo. A transformed nonconformist must turn inertia into a palpable sense of urgency. Urgency forces us to answer the questions "why now?" and "why this issue?" rather than countless other issues and distractions that vie for our attention. Breaking people out of inertia often requires pricking their conscience and causing them to feel a personal connection to the victims of injustice. It also involves providing easy and accessible onramps for action to engage people further in the cause and campaign. If the bar is set too high at the onset, many people will feel overwhelmed and will balk, falling back to the safety of inertia.

The second barrier is fear, which includes the fear of real or perceived risks associated with getting in the way of injustice. We may fear fallout from colleagues, family or even friends, particularly if the issues we are getting involved in are controversial. Living a countercultural life of activism can involve persecution, particularly in countries that don't enjoy the same degree of protections for free speech and assembly as the United States. It is easy to take these freedoms for granted and forget that for billions of people across the world these freedoms are curtailed and denied on a daily basis, from China to Iran to Zimbabwe.

As much as fear can prevent engagement in activism, fear has also been used as a powerful motivator, often in destructive and manipulative ways. Hitler stoked German fears around lost prowess following World War I, targeting Jews as a convenient scapegoat. Some opponents of immigration reform have appealed to people's fear of joblessness and economic insecurity, unjustly castigating undocumented immigrants. Both of these examples illustrate the problem with appealing to fear: it causes us to turn inward and feeds off of bitterness or resentment rather than hope. Hope represents the best antidote to counteract fear. Campaigns that appeal to hope are inclusive in their aims and refuse to engage in the vicious cycle of blame and recrimination.

A third barrier is apathy. We can easily become desensitized to the pain and suffering in the world. Apathy is often fed by cynicism, the belief that nothing will really change regardless of our actions. Anger represents the best cure for apathy. In the faith context, anger is called righteous indignation toward anything that harms the sanctity of life and demeans the image of God in each of us. We naturally feel anger when people we care about are abused or persecuted. Creative maladjustment requires closing the moral distance between the people being victimized and the people you are trying to mobilize. During the early days of the Student Global AIDS Campaign, we realized that simply reciting statistics about the number of people who died every day of AIDS often had a numbing and counterproductive effect. These statistics needed a face and real story behind them. We had to explain why HIV had become a preventable and unnecessary death sentence. Young people were needlessly contracting the virus and lacked access to life-prolonging treatment due, in part, to prohibitively high drug prices and poverty. We framed the AIDS crisis as a generational cause that provided an opportunity to address longstanding issues of poverty, human rights and gender inequality. Suddenly AIDS wasn't just another issue but became a moral imperative that commanded young people's attention and action. Righteous indignation was stoked by the difference between what ought to be according to God's desires and plans and what is due to our fallen world. Closing this gap is the very heart of activism and the kingdom-building project.

The fourth barrier is self-doubt or impotence, the belief that we are powerless, under-qualified or ill-equipped to effect change. We can take heart, as many leaders in the Bible also had to overcome the same barrier. For example, Moses responds to God's call at the burning bush to lead the Israelites out of bondage with a series of questions in which he doubts his qualifications (Exodus 3–4). Moses' self-doubt is so deep that he begs God to have someone else perform the impossible mission in his place because he can't speak well. When Jeremiah hears God's call to be a "prophet to the nations," his initial response is one of self-doubt, that he does not know how to speak and is only a child (Jeremiah 1:4-9). We also often doubt that we have the courage, knowledge, training and skill set to effect change and step fully into God's purpose for our lives.

One of the most common and debilitating myths in politics is that one has to be an expert in order to be a change agent. This is particularly true in the arena of foreign policy, which tends to be much more insulated and dominated by an elite group of thinkers and actors. This is not to denigrate the critical role that knowledge, data and science play in shaping good public policy; however, democratic systems are designed to be a competitive marketplace of ideas, values and aspirations. You don't need a Ph.D. in economics to advocate effectively for a higher minimum wage, a law degree to push for reforms in our criminal system, or expertise in foreign policy to call for an end to genocide in Darfur.

A feeling of impotence often stems from the belief that our political system is too corrupt and has become impervious to outside pressure. Sadly, the proliferation of money in politics reinforces this sentiment. The cost of running a campaign has skyrocketed, forcing the majority of politicians to run a constant rat race of raising money for the next election, making them increasingly dependent on special and moneyed interests. For instance, the cost of the average congressional campaign nearly doubled from 1986 to 2006 from $706,000 to $1.345 million.[15] Fortunately, the advent of Internet-based fundraising has democratized the fundraising process; however, our system is still in desperate need of major campaign finance and lobbying reform. The Supreme Court's 2010 ruling in the Citizens United case opens up the floodgates further to corporate and union influence on campaigns. The media and lobbyists have now become powerful fourth and fifth branches of government alongside the executive, legislative and judicial. While these alarming trends curtail the impact of citizen engagement in politics, we shouldn't underestimate the power people can wield through collective action. We must be constantly reminded of the recent movements and campaigns that have transformed politics, often with meager resources and while facing incredible odds. These include ballot initiatives across the country that have increased the minimum wage; the success of the Jubilee campaign in canceling billions of dollars of debt owed by developing countries to creditors; and greater access to health care for children through the expansion of SCHIP.

One way to help people overcome self-doubt is to enable them to experience very small successes that build their confidence. This means setting very realistic and achievable goals, like challenging people to recruit one additional friend to attend the next informational meeting, then congratulating them when that goal is achieved. Good organizing requires a continual commitment to developing new leaders. The goal of a good organizer is to work themselves out of a job so that others are able to perform the same role and take on greater responsibility.

As people of faith, we are often uneasy about power and blind to the power we possess. While it is important to remember Lord Acton's dictum that "power tends to corrupt and absolute power corrupts absolutely," we are often overly timid and passive about using our God-given power because power takes on an overly negative connotation. But power can be used for life-affirming or life-denying purposes. Dr. King said it best: "power without love is reckless and abusive. Love without power is shallow and anemic. Power at its best is love implementing the demands of justice."[16] Just as the apostle Paul tells us that there are various forms of spiritual gifts, there are also various types of power. We exercise power through our money or assets, our authority, our relationships and connections, our information and knowledge, our spiritual identity, and through culture and traditions. The real question we must constantly ask ourselves is whether the purposes and motives behind our use of power are aligned with God's kingdom. Do they protect human dignity, expand opportunity and lead to more abundant life?

The last barrier is a feeling of isolation, which makes people feel alone and alienated from people who share similar interests and values.[17] In any campus, workplace, church, and so on, are countless people who are waiting for the right call to action to be drawn out of their isolation. Without an invitation we often fail to realize the degree to which other people share our values and desire to build a better community and world.

The church at its best represents an incredible vehicle for breaking people out of isolation. Built into the DNA of the church is *dia-*

konia, or service to others. The earliest church demonstrated this commitment by sharing everything in common according to need. While we may not exhibit this same radical commitment, we must find ways to break outside the four walls of the church to extend God's call to steadfast love and justice to our community and world. Churches and campus ministries are called to build a deep sense of community, fostering bonds of friendship, solidarity and shared vision. Many churches go to great lengths to remain apolitical, operating under the belief that engaging in social and political issues will automatically divide and distract their members. While engaging in politics in inappropriate, overly partisan or ideological ways represents a legitimate concern, churches that have nothing to say about the social, economic and political sphere of life overly limit God and confine the scope of ministry.

APPLYING THE CHARACTER OF CAMPAIGNS TO PREDATORY LENDING

Brian Swarts is a transformed nonconformist who helped lead a pioneering campaign against predatory lending in Oregon. According to Swarts, "the state of Oregon has become well known for a number of things in recent years including a Starbucks on nearly every corner, top chefs who are picking up and leaving places like New York and LA to settle in Portland, and more microbreweries per capita than any other state. Yet, up until 2007, Oregon had one of the biggest problems with predatory payday lending in the country, having more check-cashing and payday loan shops than McDonald's restaurants."[18] Brian recruited churches to join the Economic Fairness Coalition, which led a campaign to take on this modern day form of usury.

First, the campaign had to evaluate and judge the nature, scope and root causes of the predatory lending crisis. Campaign leaders found that the lending practices of these businesses, which cash checks for people who cannot open bank accounts and provide quick loans for those struggling to make ends meet each month, were forcing already vulnerable people into a vicious cycle of debt. These businesses were setting up shop in the most depressed areas of a community—near housing projects, migrant-worker communities and even military bases. The businesses were "banking" on the fact that financially deprived families will use their services out of desperation, even as they charge usurious interest rates that often exceed 100 or, in some cases, 300 percent. The most predatory aspect of the business is not the rates alone but the fact that the rates are routinely used to trap people into a destructive cycle of debt that they cannot escape. A customer may take out a loan for an emergency car repair, to purchase medication or just to pay bills during a bad month, but the interest rates are so high that many of them cannot fully repay their loan in time and are forced to take out a second loan simply to pay off the first. Addressing the root cause required banning these usurious interest rates. Advocates in Oregon did their research and found that over 60 percent of borrowers had taken out at least thirteen loans during the past year with some predatory lending victims seeing a $150 payday loan transformed into more than $2000 in insurmountable debt.

In formulating their strategy, the campaign learned from other states, including North Carolina, where economic justice advocates took action to put an end to these immoral businesses in their backyards. The coalition began promoting legislation to put a cap on usurious interest rates. The campaign realized early on that it needed to build a broader coalition and that the faith community was a natural ally in this campaign. For one thing, the churches were the places many victims were turning to for comfort and aid. When the leaders of the coalition began mobilizing community members to join their campaign against predatory lending, pastors and other people of faith began coming forward with the stories of parishioners and friends whose lives were being torn apart by debt and bankruptcy. Second, the morality of the issue was self-evident to people of faith. This moral imperative helped to break the public out of its apathy around this issue. The idea of exploiting people in need, including the elderly, in such a blatant way not only seemed wrong, it was in direct contradiction to Scripture.

Christianity, Judaism and Islam all carry clear teachings against usury and depict stories of those who exploit the poor and marginalized. The Economic Fairness Coalition turned to faith leaders and communities for help. In coordination with three faith-based advocacy coalitions, the Oregon Faith Roundtable Against Hunger (OFRAH), Ecumenical Ministries of Oregon (EMO) and the Oregon Center for Christian Values (OCCV), the campaign was able to share its vision directly with believers in the pews.

This broad coalition devised a series of tactics to generate greater public awareness and galvanize public pressure against these practices, including a massive, statewide postcard-writing campaign; phone calls and visits with their elected leaders; and the sharing of testimonies directly with members of the legislature during hearings at the state capitol in Salem. The response was overwhelming, as the general public became outraged to learn how vulnerable citizens and families were being exploited in their state. Christians from across the spectrum got involved, from Catholics to mainline Protestants to evangelicals as well as numerous Jewish and Muslim groups. The power of the campaign was that the moral issue was so clear. It became a teachable moment for people to see how faith really can and must intersect with the common good in a community.

Campaign leaders came to a consensus that they needed a visible champion to step up and show moral leadership on the issue. Jeff Merkley, then Speaker of the House for the state of Oregon, was identified and recruited as the ideal candidate. Merkley, a devout Christian with a deep sense of his moral calling in public life, had served as the director of Habitat for Humanity in Portland, where he became very familiar with the struggles of families who were being preyed upon by loan sharks. Merkley was asked to put his political capital and reputation on the line behind the legislation. While there was little political advantage for him in this effort since in the beginning no one really knew anything about the bill, the moral imperative and broad coalition proved persuasive.

Owners of the payday loan stores in Oregon were part of a billion-dollar corporation that owned stores all over the country and was prepared to spend millions to stop the campaign. While it wielded a substantial financial advantage, the moral choice was stark. In the end, the united voice of thousands of people of faith from across the state and the unwavering support of the most powerful leader in the legislature brought an unexpected, but not unprecedented, victory. The campaign illustrates that money and power do not always have the upper hand, particularly when up against the passion and conviction of people who are united behind a higher calling. It is not only the outcome but the solidarity and pride generated by people of faith coming together for justice that makes it such a powerful force for good in society. Since they won the campaign in Oregon, numerous other states have been inspired to put an end to predatory lending practices in their own backyards. Merkley is now the newest U.S. Senator from Oregon—yet again showing that strong moral leadership can lead to greater things.

MODELING THE PERSISTENT WIDOW

So often we want and expect change to take place overnight; however, more often than not, moving mountains of injustice requires dogged persistence and a long-term commitment. When I grow impatient or weary I remember the parable of the persistent widow (Luke 18:1-8), which provides a powerful window into the biblical call to both advocacy and organizing. In the parable, a widow seeks justice from a judge who neither fears nor loves God. We aren't told the exact nature of the woman's grievance. However, we know that some kind of injustice has been committed against her.

During the time of Christ, widows were one of the most marginalized groups within society; they were often denied property rights, lived in poverty and were often scorned by the rest of society. Yet this widow refuses to give up despite the judge's obstinacy and indifference. The widow goes back to the judge multiple times in order to argue her case. I can picture the widow appealing to the judge's faith, then his conscience and finally his self-interest. Even as each of these approaches fails, her sheer persistence wears down the judge's will and ultimately forces him to grant her justice.

In the context of social and political change, we too must be as persistent and resilient as the widow. Too often we underestimate the power we wield and tolerate conditions and circumstances that we have the ability to change if we are willing to be as relentless and determined as the widow. Walls of injustice almost never come down overnight. Entrenched and powerful interests keep these walls intact. I don't believe it is arbitrary that Jesus chose a widow to be the heroine in this parable. In describing the ability of a widow to seek and secure justice from a powerful judge, Jesus was sending a powerful message to all of ancient Israel that they too had the power to secure justice. If a disenfranchised and disinherited widow could secure justice, then certainly God can use each and every one of us.

MARKERS OF THE TRANSFORMED NONCONFORMIST

Activism can be intimidating, particularly when you think about the complexity and seeming intractability of many of the injustices in the world. Where does one start? What are the best entry points? This chapter outlined some of the tools for building successful campaigns. However, transformed nonconformism doesn't start and end with campaigns. Creative maladjustment involves a broad range of daily-life commitments. At its core, it requires making a daily commitment to what Gandhi described as "being the change you want to see in the world." Our actions must become a mirror image of our core values and convictions.

Mobilizing hope can best be understood in the spiritual context of stewardship. The good news for those of us who are in debt or are financially strapped is that stewardship is about far more than money. We are called to be good stewards not simply of our money but also of our time and our talents. Creative maladjustment entails a more holistic and radical stewardship of our time and resources. Faithful stewardship is at the very heart of discipleship.

Financial stewardship. Financial stewardship often gets reduced to the Old Testament mandate to tithe 10 percent of our income to the church. The tithe is meant to be a floor on our giving, not a ceiling. In reality, everything we have and receive is a gift from God. Our personal budgets should represent a moral document, demonstrating what we value and our willingness to sacrifice on behalf of others. In addition to tithing to a local church, we can become more creative about the types of organizations that we are giving to. In line with a commitment to both charity and justice, consider contributing to organizations that help meet immediate needs as well as organizations that work to address the root causes of those needs. Leading into Christmas each year, an international movement called the Advent Conspiracy seeks to restore the "scandal" of Christmas by substituting compassion for consumption. The degree to which Christmas has become overly commercialized often overshadows the actual reason why we celebrate the day, to honor the birth of our Savior. By worshiping fully, spending less, saving more and loving others more intensely, the Advent Conspiracy seeks a better model of the true spirit of Christmas.[19]

According to a 2007 Barna Group survey, only 9 percent of self-professed born-again Christians tithed a full 10 percent of their income. Ron Sider of Evangelicals for Social Action cites a statistic that if every American Christian actually tithed a full 10 percent of their income, we would have another $143 billion available to empower the poor and spread the gospel.[20] Therefore, there is exponential room for growth in how we dedicate our earnings and our resources for serving God's purposes in the world.

Civic stewardship. The very act of voting represents an important form of transformed nonconformism that can be easily taken for granted. While our political choices will always be imperfect, we must use our best prudential judgment in selecting candidates that are the most qualified and best embody our values. Nonvoting becomes a tacit approval of whoever is elected to represent us. Voting is the very currency of our politics. It is far too easy to become cynical about our politics and lose faith in the impact of our vote. In these moments, we should pause to think about the degree to which the right to vote is still denied or curtailed in so many places around the world.

We must also work to support reforms that limit the corrosive influence of money in our political system. Since the cost of running a successful campaign has skyrocketed, candidates are increasingly caught up in fundraising rather than legislating and leading. According to the Campaign Finance Institute, the average congressional campaign continues to rise year after year due to the increasing costs of advertising and air time.[21] Greater access to public financing would help to even this playing field. We can also support efforts to make voting more accessible, such as making election day a federal holiday or eliminating laws in many states that disenfranchise former inmates who have already repaid their debt to society.

Civic stewardship doesn't end with voting. It also involves building a relationship with elected representatives by making and keeping contact with them. When citizens become disillusioned and disengaged, politicians lack the mechanisms for real accountability. You have far more access than you realize.

Have you ever considered running for an elected office? Whether

it's a local school board, building association or congressional office, civic stewardship is measured by how we use our voice and
influence to impact our government and public policy. From can-
vassing for candidates we believe in, to writing letters or emails, to
fundraising, to writing op-eds, to voting and even seeking office
ourselves, an engaged and active citizenry represents the lifeblood
of democracy and the core of civic stewardship.

Consumer stewardship. Hosea 4:6 reminds us that "people
are destroyed from lack of knowledge." Due to the increasingly
opaque and complex nature of the global economy, we often lack
knowledge of how products are made, where they come from, and
what the practices and values are of the corporations that produced them. The irony is that we have much greater *access* to information today than ever before about the conditions under
which the products we buy are produced. Yet we have to be willing to do our homework and expend the extra effort. What we
buy and where we shop are not simply economic or consumer decisions; they are also deeply spiritual ones. Creative maladjustment means caring as much about the ingredients within products as the process by which they came to the market, from the
labor that was used to produce them to their impact on the environment. Every time we enter a shopping mall, grocery store or
gas station, we are making consumer choices that have profound
moral implications.

We have only scratched the surface of our consumer-based
power. In an age in which corporations shape so much of our
lives and influence so much of our politics, consumer activism is
more critical than ever before. Famous actions like the 1955-1956
boycott of public buses in Montgomery, Alabama, and the boycott of grapes during the mid-1960s farm-workers campaign in
California demonstrate the power of consumer choices and solidarity. In more recent times, the conflict diamond campaign
pressured major diamond distributors to stop buying diamonds

smuggled from countries in which the diamond trade fueled bloody conflicts.

Many churches and college campuses are responding to this call to consumer stewardship, investing only in socially responsible mutual funds and stocks, and only purchasing fair-trade-certified products—products that are not made under exploitative conditions and that ensure a just share of the profits actually reach the actual producer, whether it's the farmer growing coffee or the village artisan weaving a basket. (The fair trade movement in the United States trails efforts in the United Kingdom, where, thanks to the popular education of campaigns by organizations like TradeCraft, as much as 20 percent of products purchased in grocery stores are fair trade certified.) While buying fair trade products doesn't replace the need for advocacy to right unjust trade policies, it represents a small ripple in a larger ocean of building right relationships.

Environmental stewardship. Creation care has made incredible inroads in the Christian world, premised on the belief that we are called to be responsible and good stewards of God's creation. The environmental movement was once typecast as being dominated by radical tree huggers and animal rights activists who wanted to force everyone to become a vegetarian. But today these stereotypes no longer hold, as it has become more clear that everyone needs to practice environmental responsibility. America's consumption habits and overdependence on oil and carbon distorts our foreign policy and places the nation on an unsustainable trajectory, accelerating global climate change that will disproportionately hurt the countries of the world who have the smallest carbon footprints. A shift from carbon to renewable sources of energy has become an environmental and an economic imperative.

There are hundreds of simple actions we can take to become better environmental stewards. The Environmental Protection Agency offers a laundry list of easy and effective ways to reduce pollution and enhance healthy living. Christians might make a Lenten commitment to give up purchasing any "new" goods beyond the daily necessities (food, hygiene, etc.). As we live with less, we often learn that we already have much more than we ever needed. I have a great deal to learn about how to live a more environmentally conscious and friendly lifestyle. But whether by driving less, walking more, recycling, eating less meat, using less electricity, or insulating or retrofitting our homes, our acts of environmental stewardship create a ripple effect with profound earth-sustaining consequences.

Relational stewardship. The breadth, depth and diversity of our relationships say a great deal about our faith and our values. We are called to love our neighbor as ourselves. It is often easier to love our neighbors when they share the same background and values; however, we are called to stretch beyond our comfort zone and love even the neighbors that are most foreign or difficult to love. Our relationships become a living testimony of whom and what we value. The farther we extend this circle of relational capital, the more people will be touched by our altruism and benevolence.

I've learned a great deal about the power of relational stewardship through my wife's Jamaican family. The first time I visited her family in Montego Bay, I was thoroughly confused. Every adult I met was called an uncle or aunt. I quickly lost track of who was actually related to my wife by blood and who was simply a close family friend who filled in the role of a family member. Imagine if everyone had a circle that large of adults who looked out for their welfare and interest and felt a direct stake in their development and success. Relationships are the conduit through which we demonstrate our love for God.

FARAWAY JUSTICE AND LOCAL INVOLVEMENT
In 2007 the world celebrated the two-hundred-year anniversary of

the end of the Transatlantic slave trade. Its principal architect, William Wilberforce, once an unknown and largely obscure British Parliamentarian, has now been rediscovered as an inspiring advocate for justice driven by his devout faith. Wilberforce dedicated an entire lifetime to a tireless campaign to end the heinous slave trade and then to abolish slavery itself. Wilberforce's bill in Parliament to abolish slavery failed nine times before finally passing nineteen years after it was first introduced. The Slavery Abolition Bill passed in 1833, triumphing in the House of Commons three days before Wilberforce's death. Ending the brutal slave trade required a political change and solution. No amount of charity or goodwill could bring an end to the practice of slavery. In order to succeed, the campaign had to expose both the nature and the root causes of the slave trade, making a largely invisible trade starkly visible to the British people. The campaign had to overcome public ignorance and apathy as well as entrenched, powerful companies who had a vested interest in maintaining the status quo.

Wilberforce and the Clapham Group built a movement to galvanize public opinion against the slave trade by bringing horrifying images and stories of the trade into the lives of the British public and connecting the trade to their daily lives. The campaign organized a boycott against sugar and led a petition drive that generated 390,000 signatures from all across Britain. The sugar boycott helped to make the connection between faraway injustice and local consumption real. Antislavery organizers pioneered many of the tactics used today such as speaking tours, mass boycotts, voter guides and building local chapters of a national organization. Pamphleteer William Fox pointed out, "If we purchase the commodity [sugar] we participate in the crime," adding that in each pound of slave-grown sugar "we may be considered as consuming two ounces of human flesh."[22]

With such tactics, Wilberforce and the Clapham Group persuaded the British people that their private practices had far-reaching effects, and that injustice anywhere, to borrow from Dr. King, represents an injustice everywhere. In order for that same truth to be embraced today, we need to embrace not only personal steward-ship but a biblical vision of beloved community, which means re-sisting the allure and even defying our deep-seated instincts of rugged individualism.

CHAPTER 6

REDEEMING THE AMERICAN DREAM

FROM RUGGED INDIVIDUALISM TO THE BELOVED COMMUNITY

Every man must decide whether he will walk in the light of creative altruism or the darkness of destructive selfishness. This is the judgment. Life's most persistent and urgent question is, What are you doing for others?

DR. MARTIN LUTHER KING JR.

One of the teachers of the law came and heard them debating. Noticing that Jesus had given them a good answer, he asked him, "Of all the commandments, which is the most important?"

"The most important one," answered Jesus, "is this: 'Hear, O Israel, the Lord our God, the Lord is one. Love the Lord your God with all your heart and with all your soul and with all your mind and with all your strength.' The second is this: 'Love your neighbor as yourself.' There is no commandment greater than these."

MARK 12:28-31

THE AMERICAN COWBOY REPRESENTS an iconic American image. With a cigarette dangling from his mouth and lasso in hand, he epitomizes defiance, virility and self-reliance. The cowboy embodies the frontier spirit of rugged individualism, which seems ingrained in the American ethos and psyche. Rugged individualists pursue their own goals and desires while opposing most external interference on their choices. There is a positive side to this ethic, as it has fostered an American entrepreneurship and ingenuity spurring innovation and growth. The Puritan principles of prudence, hard work and temperance also tie into this ethic in positive ways.

However, the underside of individualism is far less appealing and rubs up against Christ's mandate both to be our brothers' and sisters' keeper and to love our neighbor as ourselves. Rugged individualists only embrace the first part of Rabbi Hillel's challenge that "if I am not for myself, who will be?" by looking after themselves and drawing narrow and finite lines around who constitutes their community. This myopic and provincial mentality has seeped into our economic thinking and behavior. As a result, America often suffers from an acute culture of selfishness, fueled by the false belief that we are better off when each person looks out primarily for themselves.

Rugged individualism has also crept into our theology, evangelism and sense of mission within the church. In this vein, God is primarily concerned with the lives and actions of individuals. The collective nature of who we are as a faith community becomes overshadowed by our pursuit of personal salvation, a focus that leads to a fixation on personal morality, often at the expense of public morality. The church also frequently sanctifies the pursuit of an overly materialistic life, as though God's promise for a more abundant life is synonymous with a certain level of affluence and comfort. The topic of money is too rarely preached outside the context of tithing and stewardship in the church. Instead of resisting and transforming a culture of hedonistic consumption, too often the church feeds and at times even blesses it.

Rugged individualism has seemingly infiltrated every facet of life. A streak of individualism in our foreign policy has often translated into isolationism, exceptionalism and the misuse of just war. On the domestic side, individualism has overexalted the market and led to an economy driven by conspicuous consumption. Individualism in our interpersonal relationships has led to a nation that is more and more ill equipped to manage an increasingly complex and racially diverse environment. Rugged individualism has formed the backbone of how we have pursued a goal that is also ingrained in the American psyche, the American Dream.

The idea of the American Dream was first coined in James Truslow Adams's 1931 book *Epic of America*. Adams wrote, "The American Dream is that dream of a land in which life should be better and richer and fuller for every man, with opportunity for each according to ability or achievement. . . . The American Dream that has lured tens of millions of all nations to our shores in the past century has not been a dream of material plenty, though that has doubtlessly counted heavily. It has been a dream of being able to grow to the fullest development as a man and woman, unhampered by the barriers which had slowly been erected in the older civilizations, unrepressed by social orders which had developed for the benefit of classes rather than for the simple human being of any and every class."[1] Based on Adams's description, the original intent behind the American Dream was to ingrain the ideals of mobility, freedom, security and dignity. Millions of people from across the world made huge sacrifices and overcame great odds to immigrate to America because this dream captured their imagination and resonated with their aspiration for a better life. The Statue of Liberty stands as a powerful reminder and symbol of this history, with its inscription on the interior of the pedestal reading "Give me your tired, your poor, Your huddled masses yearning to breathe free." Yet these ideals have been increasingly replaced by an overly individualized and consumer-based imposter of the American Dream that makes conspicuous consumption and ostentatious wealth its goal, often with little to no regard for the common good.

The promise and meaning behind the American Dream has also been bruised and battered by the tortured history of racism in America. The brutal history of slavery followed by Jim Crow segregation made a mockery of the American Dream for African Americans. For Native Americans displaced from their lands and killed in horrific numbers, the American Dream was more often a nightmare.

One manisfestation of the American Dream is the dream of home ownership. In 2008, the dream of owning and building equity in a home was derailed by the global financial meltdown, fueled in large part by a bubble bursting in the housing market. Home ownership provides a critical path to economic security and wealth creation; however, predatory, speculative behavior by many lenders and irresponsible decisions precipitated an epidemic of foreclosures on both homes and dreams. The degree to which riskier subprime loans were bundled and leveraged to make astronomical profits put banks at risk and threatened the stability of the entire financial system. The Center for Responsible Lending projects that 2.2 million borrowers who bought homes between 1998 and 2006 will lose their houses and up to $164 billion of wealth as a result. African American and Latino home owners are twice as likely to suffer subprime-related home foreclosures as white home owners are. African Americans and Latinos are not only more likely to have been caught in the subprime loan trap; they are also far more dependent, as a rule, on their homes as financial resources.[2]

The modern-day pursuit of the American Dream reminds me of the popular reality television show *Survivor,* in which contestants are stranded in the wilderness and compete in a series of taxing physical and mental challenges that determine whether their team will be granted immunity and saved from having to vote another teammate off the island. In order to win, players must exhibit a Darwinian, survival-of-the-fittest mindset, seeking to win at all costs, even if it requires lying and actively sabotaging their opponents. I watched my first season of *Survivor* in 2009, in large part because one of my friends and colleagues from my year in the Urban Fellows program was chosen to be one of the contestants. The show has an addictive quality as you get drawn in by the personalities and competing strategies of the competitors. I was struck by a moment at the end of the nineteenth season of the show in which the other finalists rejected a win-in-any-way-possible mentality. Russell, one of the two finalists, played the game with ruthless cunning and many underhanded tactics. He worked to turn contestants against each other, lied about his background, and made promises that he had no intention of keeping. Even though these tactics contributed to his advancement, they ultimately cost him the game because the very people who ultimately vote to name the Survivor winner are the same people Russell lied to and backstabbed. It was a refreshing reminder that even in a society that exalts the individual, communal values and virtue are still alive and valued.

THE POWER OF THE GOLDEN RULE

Instead of a survival-of-the-fittest mentality, creative maladjustment calls for a different pattern, rooted in the Golden Rule. The Golden Rule provides a necessary antidote to the overly individualistic streak in American culture. Jesus articulated a holistic conception of spirituality in this way: "You shall love the Lord your God with all your heart, and with all your soul, and with all your mind" and "You shall love your neighbor as yourself" (Matthew 22:37, 39 NRSV).[3] The Golden Rule is about more than simply treating people as you would like to be treated. It's about an abiding and deep-seated concern for the welfare of your neighbor rooted in an understanding of our mutuality and interdependence. Our vertical relationship with God empowers and calls us into a horizontal relationship with others. Our faith is never meant to be private possession but instead a contagious public good.

The Golden Rule is tested in the context of community, particularly in situations in which we have a hard time identifying with our neighbor. This includes instances when our neighbor is out of mind and sight, whether it's because they live on the other side of the railroad tracks or halfway across the world. Because the dominant images we see portrayed in the media of many communities and countries are of violence, conflict and abject poverty, we can become desensitized to these conditions, which then become normalized. In response, we must find ways to humanize the struggles and triumphs of people who face various forms of injustice. Otherwise, we are liable to view them as helpless victims or blame them for their situation, both leading down a dangerous road. Loving our neighbor as we love ourselves requires getting to know our neighbors, seeking to understand their stories, hopes and aspirations. We will likely find that we share a lot more in common than we realize.

In the work of Susan Wilkinson-Maposa and Alan Fowler, research teams asked 677 poor people from Mozambique, Namibia, South Africa and Zimbabwe five questions: What is help? Who do you help and who helps you? What forms of help are used and for what purposes? Why do you help? And has help changed over time? The answers revolutionized their understanding of what they call "horizontal philanthropy," in which people give not as a matter of free choice but out of a deep sense of mutual obligation. People living with less material wealth are often far more generous with their meager resources than affluent people are with their abundant resources. In a tragic irony, so often the excess of possessions leads to a greater unwillingness to give of ourselves sacrificially.

Too often the Golden Rule sounds like an elegant and pretty concept but feels impractical and difficult to live out in real life. The southern African concept of *Ubuntu*, a deeply felt Golden Rule–like ethic that America can learn from, provides the counterbalance and antidote to the decadence of rugged individualism.

THE GOLDEN RULE AND UBUNTU

In 1997, I spent a semester studying at the University of Cape Town through the School for International Training (SIT). While in the academic portion of the program, I volunteered at an orphanage in the heart of Langa, an impoverished township outside of Cape Town. At that time, the majority of residents lived in makeshift shacks pieced together out of corrugated metal and cardboard. Joblessness ran rampant along with malnutrition, poor health and crime.

During the orientation, I learned that the orphanage was in a state of crisis because its governing board had mismanaged funds and blamed the staff for alleged embezzlement. As a result, funding from the Baptist church abroad was pulled. In the midst of these false accusations and dried up funding the local staff made a courageous stand, refusing to leave the home until provisions were made for every orphaned child. The staff worked as caretakers for these children under a constant cloud of fear that each day would be their last at the home. The staff modeled what I imagine the early church looked like in the second chapter of Acts, in which all possessions were shared according to need. In a similar fashion, the staff shared everything they had with the kids and exhibited a fierce, sacrificial love despite their uncertain future. Their example put flesh on the philosophy of Ubuntu, otherwise known as African humanism.

Ubuntu is a way of being that is deeply embedded within southern African culture and philosophy. Simply put, Ubuntu means that "I am because we are." In other words, it is through our relationships that our lives take on greater and fuller meaning. Ubuntu is about "rootedness of the self in community," the capacity to express compassion, reciprocity, dignity, harmony and humanity in the interest of eliminating inequities and establishing and sustaining justice. Ubuntu seeks to honor human relationships as primary in any social, communal or corporate activity.[4] According to Archbishop Desmond Tutu, "a person with *ubuntu* is open and available to others, affirming of others, does not feel threatened that others are able and good, for he or she has a proper self-assurance that comes from knowing that he or she belongs in a greater whole and is diminished when others are humiliated or diminished."[5]

The staff asked me to help them raise funds to keep the orphanage open. I quickly realized that scraping together donations would only serve as a stopgap and would put a Band-Aid on what was really a crisis of deeper proportion. Without the sustained assistance from the community, these children would lose the only home they had known. Thus, in addition to the fundraising effort to meet immediate needs, we realized it was necessary to mobilize the community through a public awareness campaign. The staff and community decided that the local member of Parliament representing Langa and key leaders from the business community had the power to intervene and create a longer-term solution to keep the orphanage open. In order to capture their attention we launched a letter-writing and media campaign.

I remember a seminal moment in the life of the campaign in which the police tried to enforce a court-ordered injunction to evict the staff and orphans from the facility. News of the court injunction spread like wildfire throughout the township. The staff notified the media to be on alert to shine a spotlight on what was about to unfold. The next day police arrived with dogs and military-like trucks, an image reminiscent of the apartheid-era days, only to find hundreds of community members conducting a nonviolent sit-in at the facility. Many community members had skipped work in order to physically demonstrate their support for the staff and children. I was moved by their courage and sacrificial solidarity. The police were wise enough to know that forcing their way into the orphanage would cause an altercation and would generate a great deal of negative publicity. Instead, they gave the staff and community a few weeks to vacate the premises. The extension and the media coverage the incident generated convinced the member of Parliament representing Langa to use her political capital to intervene. Business leaders also pledged financial support while a political solution was negotiated to keep the orphanage open. The campaign demonstrated Ubuntu in action.

An ethic of Ubuntu and the rugged individualist are constantly at war inside of us, pushing and pulling us in competing directions. The ethic we choose to feed is the ethic that ultimately wins. Reverend Sharon Watkins shared this poignant Cherokee wisdom during the interfaith inauguration service for President Barack Obama. The wisdom says:

> One evening a grandfather was teaching his young grandson about the internal battle that each person faces.
>
> "There are two wolves struggling inside each of us," the old man said. "One wolf is vengefulness, anger, resentment, self-pity, fear. "The other wolf is compassion, faithfulness, hope, truth, love."
>
> The grandson sat, thinking, then asked: "Which wolf wins, Grandfather?"
>
> His grandfather replied, "The one you feed."

The question is whether we will feed the wolf of rugged individualism or of Ubuntu. In the process of feeding an ethic of Ubuntu, we can redeem the meaning and promise of the American Dream. Now is the time to dust off and embrace another metaphor and vision rooted in Ubuntu that I believe better aligns with our faith story and better captures the aspirations of the kingdom-building project: the beloved community.

THE BELOVED COMMUNITY REIMAGINED

In 2005 and 2006, I had the privilege of participating in a Binational Civil Society Forum that brought together forty leaders from across different parts of civil society in both South Africa and America. Ambassador James Joseph, who served as the ambassador to South Africa under the Clinton administration, initially conceived of the forum during his ambassadorship. Ambassador Joseph was able to make this dream become a reality years later. The overarching question that animated our discussions was around identifying a unifying concept that best encapsulated our understanding of social justice. In other words, what is the end we are seeking to achieve in South Africa and America? After a great deal of lively debate and deliberation, we kept coming back to Dr. King's concept of the beloved community.

When Dr. King described the end goal of the civil rights movement he said, "The end is reconciliation, the end is redemption, the end is the creation of the beloved community."[6] The beloved community becomes a powerful metaphor describing our interdependence and interconnectedness in the midst of the differences that so often separate us and cause us to deny responsibility to and for one another. Dr. King brilliantly placed the word *beloved* as the qualifying descriptor for the kind of community that we should be striving to achieve. Marlon Millner describes the beloved community as "one in which love of God and love of neighbor reigns. Such love is not just solidarity, but sacrificial. And we are a long way from it yet."[7]

Ubuntu provides the bridge to walk across the chasm between rugged individualism and the creation of the beloved community. Rightly practiced, Ubuntu helps to move us beyond simply securing equal rights to highlighting the internal shifts that the Golden Rule demands. A generous and magnanimous spirit is not something that can be legislated or prescribed. Thus, a concern and regard for the welfare of our neighbor must become rooted in our values, our daily interactions and our actions.

The Community Development Corporation (CDC) movement provides an example of Ubuntu in action. CDCs have exploded across the country. In 1970 there were roughly 100 CDCs across the United States; by 2006 there were 4600 that cumulatively produced 1.25 million homes, 126 million square feet of commercial/industrial space and 774,000 jobs. CDCs are controlled by a board of directors composed of community members, providing a laboratory for leadership development and community ownership.[8] The Christian Community Development Association (CCDA) represents a prime example. CCDA is a growing movement of churches and faith-based organizations that are engaging in local efforts to empower their communities based on founder John Perkins's three pioneering principles of relocation, redistribution and reconciliation. Perkins believes this trinity of disciplines illuminates areas where the civil rights movement failed to deliver on its most basic promises of solidarity with the poor: black economic power and racial reconciliation.[9] CCDA president Dr. Wayne Gordon captures the essence of this approach when he writes:

> The most creative long-term solutions to the problems of the poor are coming from grassroots and church-based efforts. The solutions are coming from people who see themselves as the replacements, the agents, for Jesus here on earth, in their own neighborhoods and communities. This philosophy is known as Christian Community Development, which is not a concept that was developed in a classroom, nor formulated by people foreign to the poor community. These are Biblical, practical principles evolved from years of living and working among the poor. . . . Relocation transforms "you, them, and theirs" to "we, us, and ours." Effective ministries plant and build communities of believers that have a personal stake in the development of their neighborhoods. . . . Christian Com-

munity Development is intentional about reconciliation and works hard to bring people of all races and cultures into the one worshipping body of Christ. . . . Redistribution brings new skills, new relationships, and new resources and puts them to work to empower the residents of a given community of need to bring about healthy transformation.[10]

What's often missing from these three Rs is an emphasis on changing unjust public policies. Fortunately, the pendulum within the CCDA movement is shifting toward embracing the need for advocacy for systemic change. I had the honor and privilege of helping to design and lead an advocacy track at the 2006 and 2007 CCDA national conferences. While the focus of the conference was still clearly on community development and incarnational ministry, leaders were receptive to the call for more just public policy. CCDA leaders are some of the most credible and persuasive advocates because they can offer a firsthand account of the effects of neglect, disinvestment and failed public policies within their communities. Adding a fourth commitment to systemic and structural change provides a powerful set of tools for building the beloved community. However, in order to get there, we must recognize that the landscape for social and political change has changed in fundamental ways. Thus, transformed nonconformists need new wine that matches this new reality in order to be effective change agents.

CHAPTER 7
NEW WINE FOR A CHANGED WORLD

IN JANUARY 2010 I ATTENDED A Dr. Martin Luther King memorial service at Alfred St. Baptist Church in Alexandria, Virginia. The youth of the church put on a theatrical overview of the civil rights movement to commemorate Dr. King's life and celebrate his legacy. They acted out pivotal moments in the civil rights movement, from the first student sit-in in Greensboro, North Carolina, to the bus boycott in Montgomery to the March on Washington and the sanitation-worker strike in Memphis, Tennessee. As I watched middle and high school students deliver speeches and act out scenes from the movement, I was filled with an overwhelming sense of hope. I felt as though the torch had been passed to a new generation of young people who understand the shoulders upon which they stand and the unfinished business that lies before them. Yet I wondered whether they fully grasped the degree to which the world had changed since the height of the civil rights struggle. There's a risk in overly memorializing and romanticizing the civil rights struggle in ways that get us stuck in old paradigms. Sadly, America's recent trajectory has led to an increasingly unequal, re-segregated America while missing a window of opportunity to offer bold moral leadership in an increasingly integrated and interdependent world.

Hours after the 2008 election results were announced and Barack Obama was declared the winner, an exodus of people poured out onto the 14th Street corridor in Washington, D.C., in a revelry of spontaneous and exuberant celebration. I stood in the midst of this thronging crowd sharing hugs, high fives and fist bumps with random strangers from seemingly every racial and ethnic background. In that instant the crowd felt like a family reunion of long lost brothers and sisters. We stood on top of the hallowed ashes of a Columbia Heights and U Street neighborhood that had burned to the ground forty years earlier after news of Dr. King's assassination in Memphis reached the rest of the country. On the same ground destroyed by rage arose newfound unity and hope. Regardless of how you voted, that night was a poignant moment in America's history.

We shouldn't lose sight of the symbolism that just forty years earlier in 1968, America experienced a tragic turning point in its history. Dr. King's assassination in Memphis and Robert Kennedy's assassination in Los Angeles on the eve of a major primary victory derailed the civil rights movement's pursuit of the beloved community. A fervent dedication to nonviolent social protest and a vision of an integrated movement was replaced by the anger of black power and separatism. The Vietnam War diverted America's attention away from the struggle for economic justice, siphoning massive financial resources and taking the political wind out of the sails of President Lyndon Johnson's Great Society programs. American politics became increasingly divided along the lines of a culture war that also fractured the church, creating a greater divide between mainline and evangelical churches. Abortion, school prayer and family values became the rallying cry of a conservative religious movement, leading to the creation of organizations like the Moral Majority and Christian Coalition and causing a realignment in American politics around issues of values and personal morality. Meanwhile the free market became a new religion, with Reagan's emphasis on trickle-down economics and unbridled support for small government and deregulation.

Forty years later we face a new set of realities as our world has changed in critical ways. First is the alarming trend that the economy is characterized by increasing inequality and rising levels of poverty. The spoils of economic growth have been unequally shared, with minimal gains and rising strain on the bottom and middle. Market values have seeped into every aspect of our lives. The Great Recession that began in 2008 provides a potential *kairos* moment to reimagine and restructure our economy according to a new ethic aligned with the biblical notion of jubilee.

Second, we see a backlash to many of the programs that were set up to make amends for our tortured racial history. In the context of President Obama's historic election, many people have been quick to embrace a misleading myth that we have become a postracial America. An eroding commitment to both racial reconciliation and justice comes at our own peril, particularly as our nation's schools and neighborhoods resegregate along racial and class lines and our nation approaches a watershed moment forecasted for 2042 in which racial minority groups will be in the majority.

Third, we must grapple with the newfound reality that the challenges and threats we face are increasingly transnational in nature, whether it is global climate change, human trafficking or terrorism. These and other threats require bolder global leadership and greater international cooperation.

In order to pick up where the civil rights movement left off and take our nation on a different course, new wine or new paradigms are needed that fit our contemporary context and reality. Transformed nonconformists will need this new wine as old paradigms have become outdated. These new paradigms include (1) a jubilee ethic to help provide a moral compass for our economy; (2) a renewed commitment to racial justice and reconciliation that helps us live into an intercultural reality and (3) a foreign policy that practices and values global citizenship. A moral economy requires a renewed commitment to fighting poverty both in the United States and across the world. The economy is in dire need of a new ethic that provides a moral compass to offset the danger of greed and the failures of market fundamentalism. A moral economy will also require reforms to our financial architecture and system. A renewed commitment to racial justice and reconciliation will require bolder investments in education, job training, fair wages and so on, and healing the internalized racism that so often impedes progress. Finally, we need global leadership that prioritizes human rights, reforms international institutions and combats transnational threats.

FROM MARKET FUNDAMENTALISM TO A MORAL ECONOMY

Dr. King had the foresight to understand that economic opportunity and justice represented the next frontier of the civil rights struggle. We've inherited this unfinished business. Unfortunately we often freeze frame Dr. King in his famous "I Have a Dream" speech. In the process of celebrating and commemorating his birthday each year, Americans often overly domesticate and sanitize his message, embracing only one part of his dream. We often lionize the Dr. King of Montgomery and Selma but suffer from a case of amnesia about the Dr. King of Memphis.

The year 2008 marked the fortieth anniversary of Dr. King's assassination while he was supporting sanitation workers fighting for a living wage in Memphis and the year Robert F. Kennedy was gunned down while campaigning for president on an economic justice platform across the South and Appalachia. The year was a tragic turning point, a crossroads moment in which the aspirations of the civil rights struggle were shattered. In 1968, the Poor People's Campaign that Dr. King spearheaded before his tragic death became deluged by rain and overshadowed by riots that fanned out across the nation, destroying the commercial corridor of the Columbia Heights neighborhood in Washington, D.C., where I currently live. It has felt like forty years of wandering in the wilderness when it comes to securing economic opportunity and justice for all Americans. While there have been modest and fluctuating gains in the fight against poverty, in 2008 nearly forty million Americans were living in the quicksand of poverty, the exact same absolute number as in 1968. This translates into one out of every eight families and one in four black families.

In relation to paying fair wages, our nation has actually lost ground. When adjusted for inflation, the minimum wage was worth nearly $10 an hour in 1968. In July 2009, Congress increased the national minimum wage to $7.25. Thus, people are paid less today than in 1968, despite the escalating costs of living. While the minimum wage is not a silver bullet or a panacea to ending poverty, it represents a critical first step. A minimum wage that keeps people stuck in poverty instead of helping to get them out dispels the conservative myth that if you work full time you will not be poor. Stagnant wages undermine the argument that people should be able to lift themselves up by their own bootstraps. Low wages force too many parents to work two or three jobs, denying them precious time to be present and active parents in the lives of their children.

Hurricane Katrina had the power and potential to remove the scales from our eyes to the persistence and pervasiveness of poverty in America. The hurricane pulled the curtain on poverty in America, revealing incredible disparities of wealth and deep-seated deprivation. But the images that were flashed across our televisions seemed fleeting and easily forgotten. While the United States is the wealthiest and most powerful nation in the world, America has the ignoble distinction of having the highest proportion of children living in poverty out of all industrialized nations. The United States also has the highest incarceration rate and the greatest degree of inequality, with the gap between the "haves" and the "have-nots" dangerously approaching levels not seen since the Great Depression. More people die each year of poverty-related causes than from the combined casualties of war, natural disasters and homicide.[1] The problem is that unlike high-visibility crises, these represent silent tragedies that rarely make the headlines or the evening news. Fortunately we have the tools to effectively combat poverty. What is so often lacking is the moral and political will.

But poverty remains a third rail and almost taboo topic in politics. In the context of elections, almost every debate and speech is framed in terms of what will benefit and strengthen the American middle class. It's as though politicians have rewritten Matthew 25 to say "just as you did to the middle class you also did for me." Conventional political wisdom is that low-income Americans vote in low numbers and lack the political connections and means to contribute financially to political campaigns. Yet people of faith are called to stand in the gap for the impoverished and advocate for political decisions based on how they affect the weak and the marginalized. This is the biblical test of our civic discipleship.

IDOLATRY OF THE MARKET

Market fundamentalism is a catch-all term that describes an overdependence on the market to govern and solve societal ills. The process of rapid deregulation that characterized the past few decades has empowered corporate power beyond the capacity of the regulatory role of government. According to this dogma, markets are to be trusted as fair and impartial arbiters of exchanging goods and services. In this vein, markets free from government interference represent the key to economic prosperity. Market fundamentalism also preaches that the invisible hand of the market will maximize efficiency and, if left to its own devices, will maximize economic productivity and growth. Economic orthodoxy posits that without the incentive of unfettered profit, the economy will lack the right incentives for innovation and entrepreneurship.

In reality, the free market isn't very free. The market economy is filled with a range of double standards and rigged rules that benefit and privilege some corporations and individuals at the expense of others. For instance, agricultural subsidies that predominantly benefit large agribusinesses artificially decrease the price of staple crops at the expense of developing countries and smaller American farmers, creating an even more lopsided playing field. A pure profit motive rewards short-term gains and often enables corporations to avoid internalizing the costs associated with what economists call negative externalities. Pollution and environmental degradation often represent the most prominent examples. Many banks have engaged in excessive risk-taking that constitutes a form of gambling, except in this case, they gamble with a guarantee that the government will bail them out if they are deemed too big to fail. These contradictions in our free-market system stretch and violate the core tenets of capitalism, resulting in a rigged deck of cards governing the economy. The key is to create fair market rules that harness entrepreneurship and innovation while also serving the common good.

Market fundamentalism also feeds the way in which we measure progress and growth. Too often, growth is based on an unsustainable model of never-ending consumption without an accounting of finite natural resources. "Gross domestic product" has become the popular term used to measure a country's economic progress and health. While serving as one important economic barometer, the measure alone is deeply inadequate. The measure reflects overall growth while masking and hiding the skewed distributional impact of that growth. A great deal of the world's recent growth has been a mirage due to the way in which money is increasingly accumulated through economic transactions that have little to no bearing on real goods or services. The calamitous crash of the financial sector was based in part on this excessive risk-taking, lack of regulation and sheer greed. It was also caused by extremely complex derivatives and collateralized debt obligations, particularly credit default swaps, that camouflaged the illusionary nature of a great deal of the recent economic growth. The problem is that as soon as you raise the issue of credit default swaps, people's eyes glaze over and they quickly lose interest. These are abstract and technical issues that seem disconnected from our daily economic lives.

ANOTHER WORLD IS POSSIBLE, ANOTHER WORLD IS NECESSARY

Two groundbreaking events dramatically reshaped my understanding of the global economy: the World Trade Organization protests in Seattle in November of 1999 and the Millennial Summit in September of 2000. I watched media coverage of what became known as the "battle in Seattle" with a great deal of hope and trepidation. I was hopeful that thousands of people converging on the streets of Seattle would lift up an alternative vision of the global economy and demand a stronger ethic to counterbalance corporate power and abuse. At the same time, I was fearful that potential violence would undermine the protests and that the message would be far too muddled and messy to get through to the average American. Unfortunately, the merits of the protesters' critiques became quickly lost in the media's fixation on a minority group of anarchists who marred the protest with property destruction and violence.

The Seattle protests caught the media and world by surprise with their scale and intensity. Yet the poorly and often misnamed "antiglobalization movement" had been bubbling beneath the surface and building momentum for quite some time. In a broad sense, protesters took to the streets as a gut-level visceral reaction to the commodification of everything. "Democratic" or "just" globalization is a better and more accurate description of the movement's aims and goals.

In the summer of 2000, the United Nations hosted the Millennial Summit, which focused on ensuring that the benefits of globalization reached those countries and people most left out and left behind. One hundred eighty-nine member states of the United Nations signed a compact committing the world to a set of bold, ambitious and measurable goals called the Millennium Development Goals, the first of which was to cut in half the number of people around the globe living in extreme poverty by the year 2015. The goals represented a covenant between developed and developing countries based on the principle of mutual responsibility and interdependence. Yet without a sizable and organized global campaign, the goals initially became sounding brass and clanging symbol. Without a public education campaign to capture the support and moral imagination of the public, leaders lacked real accountability, and the goals risked joining a graveyard of broken promises by the United Nations and world leaders.

September 11 and the ill-conceived "war on terror" took the wind out of the sails of the movement for a more just and democratic globalization. Protests of the WTO, World Bank and International Monetary Fund were largely replaced by opposition to the Iraq War. The 2005 G8 Summit represented the one exception, in part because momentum had been building well before 2001 to transform the G8 Summit at Gleneagles into an accountability moment for G8 leaders to support a bold antipoverty agenda. The slogan "Make Poverty History" captured the spirit and audacity of the moment. Despite major promises that were made to double aid to Africa within five years, accelerate 100 percent debt cancellation for qualifying countries and achieve universal access to HIV treatment by 2010, these commitments were overshadowed by a terrorist attack in London that suspended the Summit proceedings for a day. Only pieces of this civil society groundswell survived, including successful campaigns to fight the global AIDS epidemic and the Jubilee campaign for debt cancellation.

In 2005 a chasm existed between the World Social Forum and

the World Economic Forum. One took place in Switzerland cost-ing thousands of dollars per participant in the remote and exclu-sive Swiss resort of Davos. The other had a sliding fee of $25 and was held in Porto Alegre, Brazil. The worlds of business and pro-gressive civil society faced off each year, putting forth very differ-ent visions of how to promote prosperity and economic develop-ment. The World Social Forum theme of "Another World Is Possible" provided a counterbalance to the World Economic Fo-rum's focus on a business-driven model.[2] Fortunately, there has been a growing convergence between these summits, particularly as the World Economic Forum invites more civil society participa-tion and broadens its agenda to include a focus on the people in the bottom billion of the world.

FROM BAD TO WORSE

In 2009, the United Nations estimated that 55 to 90 million people around the world were dragged into extreme poverty due to the global economic downturn. The Center for Budget Priorities esti-mates that an additional 9 million people will be pulled into pov-erty in the United States as a result of the recession. Already in 2008, the Census Bureau estimates that 2.5 million additional Americans fell into the quicksand of poverty. Yet the church lacks a sense of righteous indignation about the degree of inequality and preventable suffering in our midst. We have found convenient ways to excuse and rationalize the growing depths of inequality that surround us locally and globally.

As this chapter is being written, the world is beginning to re-cover from the worst financial crisis since the Great Depression. The danger in this economic recovery is that our interventions and bailouts will only end up resuscitating a Frankenstein economy. We risk simply repeating the same failed policies of the past based on the same misguided economic assumptions that helped get us into this current mess in the first place. Instead, we must reorder our economic priorities and reform a broken economic architecture. The recent economic collapse (now referred to as the Great Recession) reminds me of two social sins from Gandhi's famous seven deadly social sins. Gandhi warned about the dangers of wealth without work and commerce without morality. Presently the economy is filled with far too much of both. The average CEO now makes in one day what the average worker makes in one year of wages. Excessive risk-taking through financial speculation and complicated insurance schemes generated a great deal of illusionary wealth based on promises rather than actual products being made or services being rendered. In today's market, this phantom wealth, particularly in the context of the overheated housing market, generated a bubble that has had a profound, destabilizing ripple effect across the economy. The regulatory reform bills still being debated as of May 2010 in Congress represent a long-overdue effort to bring greater sanity, accountability and responsibility back into the financial system.

A JUBILEE ECONOMY

The biblical concept of jubilee provides a needed corrective to the excesses and limitations of market fundamentalism. The jubilee economy is based on the simple but powerful notion of restoring and building right relationships. The Sabbath and Jubilee commandments deal with the way in which people are to relate to each other and to the land in the context of their relationship with God. The notion behind Jubilee recognizes that the economy will inexorably lead to the concentration of wealth in too few hands. Practicing the Jubilee year provides a periodic recalibration of economic relationships.

Leviticus 25 introduces the Jubilee year, a year that follows seven cycles of sabbath years. Ever seventh year, or the sabbath year, the land was to enjoy a rest and the crops that grew on their own were to be left for the poor and wild animals (Exodus 23:11).

In the fiftieth year or Jubilee year, all debts which had been incurred to fellow Israelites were also to be canceled (Deuteronomy 15:1-11). Part of the unique and meaningful character of the Jubilee and Sabbath commandments was that God took these known concepts, combined them and instituted them to be a permanent pattern in the life of Israel. In this way liberation and restoration were to become built in to the fabric of society.

While there is no evidence that the biblical jubilee was ever fully carried out in ancient Israel, it is quite possible that these commands were observed by groups of people at various times. Although it is not specifically mentioned in Acts, the first church at Jerusalem modeled the meaning of the jubilee commandment, for "all the believers were one in heart and mind. No one claimed that any of his possessions was his own, but they shared everything they had. With great power the apostles continued to testify to the resurrection of the Lord Jesus, and much grace was upon them all. There were no needy persons among them. For from time to time those who owned lands or houses sold them, brought the money from the sales and put it at the apostles' feet, and it was distributed to anyone as he had need" (Acts 4:32-35).[3]

The Jubilee year responds to the ways in which wealth naturally and inexorably concentrates in the hands of the few, often at the expense of the many. While this seems to be a law of economics and of human nature, this is not God's desire and is inconsistent with the ways of God's kingdom. Imagine if we put in place a random, periodic Jubilee every fifty years? No one could know the time or date in which the Jubilee was going to be put into effect in order to prevent excessive risk-taking or gaming of the system just prior to the Jubilee year. This is obviously an extreme and unrealistic proposal; however, it helps to illustrate just how radical the application of the Jubilee year would be.

The point of a Jubilee economy is to steer society toward placing the emphasis on advancing the common good and protecting the most weak and vulnerable among us, a blatant counterweight to the ethic of market fundamentalism. Catholic social teaching says that the economy exists for the person and not the person for the economy. This requires moving beyond the limited and often misleading measurement of economic growth and instead putting the emphasis on human welfare. Alongside the dominant economic measure of the gross domestic product, in a Jubilee economy we must add a COWS index (Children, Orphans, Widows/Women and Strangers/Immigrants Index).[4] This index would measure how the most marginalized people in our society are faring. In biblical times these were the widow, the orphan and the stranger. Alongside economic growth, politicians and economists must pay greater attention to human development. The United Nations Development Program produces an index each year ranking countries based on health, measured by life expectancy at birth; knowledge, measured by a combination of the adult literacy rate and the combined primary, secondary and tertiary gross enrollment ratio; and standard of living by GDP per capita. While imperfect, the human development index provides a more comprehensive picture of development beyond the often narrow and misleading indicator of growth alone.[5] Despite being the wealthiest country in absolute terms, based on 2009 UN data, the United States human development index ranked thirteenth in the world, behind Canada, Australia, Japan and Ireland.

Transforming our global economy according to a Jubilee ethic will require moving from a posture of paternalism and dependency to one of partnership and empowerment. Fledgling global trade negotiations must be revived and taken off life support. The interests of developing countries appear to be diametrically opposed to those of the United States and the European Union, due to disagreements over controversial and hypocritical subsidies on key agricultural goods and protections on intellectual property rights. The current global trade imbalance serves as a major impediment to growth in developing countries. The threefold agenda of debt cancellation, dramatically increased and reformed aid, and more just trade policies continues to be an indispensable agenda for helping countries climb the ladder of sustainable economic development.

A jubilee economy reflects the growing reality that our fates are tied together. The prophet Isaiah offers God's vision of an alternative and preferred economy. In Isaiah 65:17-24, the prophet says,

> Behold, I will create new heavens and a new earth. The former things will not be remembered, nor will they come to mind. But be glad and rejoice forever in what I will create, for I will create Jerusalem to be a delight and its people a joy. I will rejoice over Jerusalem and take delight in my people; the sound of weeping and of crying will be heard in it no more. Never again will there be in it an infant who lives but a few days, or an old man who does not live out his years; he who dies at a hundred will be thought a mere youth; he who fails to reach a hundred will be considered accursed. They will build houses and dwell in them; they will plant vineyards and eat their fruit. No longer will they build houses and others live in them, or plant and others eat. For as the days of a tree, so will be the days of my people; my chosen ones will long enjoy the works of their hands. They will not toil in vain or bear children doomed to misfortune; for they will be a people blessed by the LORD, they and their descendants with them. Before they call I will answer; while they are still speaking I will hear.

Imagine an economy that properly and fairly rewards work, ensures that everyone has access to quality health care, guarantees that every child is able to realize their full potential, and erases the pain associated with hunger and deprivation. This dream need not be utopian or a pipedream. Instead, this is God's intention and promise. It must become our conviction and aspiration as well.

CHAPTER 8

RACIAL RECONCILIATION AND RACIAL JUSTICE

THE 1989 SPIKE LEE MOVIE *Do the Right Thing* is one of my favorite films. This provocative film portrays the combustible nature of racial tensions on a blazingly hot day in Bedford-Stuyvesant, Brooklyn. The film was ahead of its time in exposing the racial friction that brews beneath the surface of American social life. When the film came out in 1989, multiethnic neighborhoods like Bedford-Stuyvesant were the exception rather than the rule across the country. Yet many cities across the South and Midwest are increasingly getting a taste of the multicultural reality that cities like New York, Miami, Los Angeles and Washington, D.C., have known for quite some time. While American cities and communities are becoming more diverse, paradoxically the majority are also growing more segregated, particularly in the context of the education system.

In his 1903 groundbreaking book *The Souls of Black Folk*, W. E. B. DuBois made the prescient statement that "the problem of the twentieth century would be the problem of the color line."[1] Racism became a dominant undercurrent and theme of the twentieth century as America struggled to extend its creed that "we hold these truths to be self-evident, that all men [and women] are created equal" to all Americans regardless of race. While our nation has made remarkable progress since 1903 in the context of dismantling racial discrimination and injustice, we cannot afford to hail racial progress at the expense of continued racial pain. A renewed commitment to racial reconciliation and justice is necessary to ensure that the problem of the twenty-first century doesn't continue to be the problem of the color line.

The demographics of our nation are changing like shifting sand, much faster than our ability to effectively manage and embrace racial and cultural differences. By the year 2042, racial and ethnic minorities will be in the majority in the United States. Some Americans look forward to this milestone with a sense of excitement and anticipation while others feel a sense of unease and trepidation. The racial demographics of America are on the move, while our sense of community has remained far too static.

It is now outdated to talk in binary terms of a white and black America. There is a rapidly growing Latino America that possesses a great deal of heterogeneity. Latinos have already surpassed African Americans as the largest minority group. Even within the "black" community, a great deal of diversity exists between first and second generation immigrants from Africa or the Caribbean compared to African Americans that have known nothing but America as their home.

In *Two Nations: Black and White, Separate, Hostile, Unequal* Andrew Hacker argues that "every one of us could write a book about race. The text is already imprinted in our minds and evokes our moral character."[2] Race in America has grown much more complex and multilayered. Our individual identities present us with "privilege" in some circumstances and with "exclusion" in others. Race shapes where we live and whom we live with, where we send our children to school, who we most naturally befriend and the likelihood of having access to wealth and health. Race also shapes how we value ourselves, who we trust, and provides quick stereotypes by which to classify people.[3]

Race impacts where and how we worship. The church hour continues to be one of the most segregated hours in American life. If a racially mixed congregation is defined as one in which no one racial group is 80 percent or more of the congregation, just 7.5 percent of the more than 300,000 religious congregations in the United States are racially mixed.[4] While predominantly black, white or Latino hours of worship will likely be permanent fixtures in the social fabric for quite some time, all congregations must make greater efforts to build bridges and strengthen relationships across this divide.

MISDIAGNOSIS: THE MYTH OF A POSTRACIAL AMERICA

During the course of the 2008 election, young people at a number of Obama rallies in Iowa started the chant "race doesn't matter." It wasn't clear whether this represented an aspiration or a pronouncement of present-day reality. Either way, the statement, while hopeful, is ultimately naive and short-sighted.

The election of Barack Obama as America's first black president validated the term a "postracial America" in the minds of many pundits and prognosticators. A "postracial America" is one in which race no longer holds any significance or sway. According to this view, racial differences have become obsolete because we have realized a misconstrued version of Dr. King's dream in which people are no longer "judged by the color of their skin but by the content of their character." By this logic, a black man becoming president of the United States signifies that the barriers blocking minority advancement have been sufficiently dismantled. President Obama's electoral victory did represent a major milestone in the journey toward racial justice, one that shouldn't be understated. In my sanctified imagination I can see countless civil rights leaders leaning over the balcony of heaven cheering loudly and beaming brightly the moment he took his oath of office. However, this achievement for our nation can't be equated with reaching the Promised Land, particularly as long as the nation remains so divided and unequal along racial lines. In reality, most white Americans voted for John McCain in the 2008 election. In fact, Barack Obama lost the white vote in 2008 by a landslide. While Obama won the overall vote by 53 percent to 46 percent, he lost among white voters by 55 percent to 43 percent.[5] Thus even by this seriously flawed yardstick of racial progress, our nation has further to go.

In the midst of President Obama's first year in office, we have seen a series of dustups over race and race relations. Despite the Obama administration's best effort to downplay racial issues and govern in a way that makes all racial groups feel represented, race still undergirds our political conversation and landscape. In a meeting at the White House, referred to as the "beer summit," President Obama tried to bridge this divide, hosting a dialogue between Professor Henry Louis Gates and Massachusetts Police Sergeant James Crowley, a white Cambridge police sergeant who arrested Gates in his own home for disorderly conduct. While the summit failed to yield an apology on either side and revealed few insights into how to defuse racial misunderstanding or prevent racial profiling, it provided a window into the nation's continued fixation and troubles with race. Another blow up took place in January 2010 based on a comment by Senator Harry Reid that came to light. Senator Reid was quoted as being "wowed by Obama's oratorical gifts and believed that the country was ready to embrace a black presidential candidate, especially one such as Obama—a 'light-skinned' African American 'with no Negro dialect, unless he wanted to have one.'"[6] After Senator Reid issued a public apology, President Obama quickly dismissed the incident as a poor choice of words. The statement was at best insensitive though not malevolent in intent.

These two examples illustrate that the media's treatment of race often focuses on the derogatory racial remarks made by public leaders. While we shouldn't tolerate racially degrading and insensitive remarks in politics or life, the amount of attention these remarks receive often overshadows a deeper set of structural inequalities that still infect America. Structural barriers, which block and impede people of color from advancing and succeeding compared to white Americans, play a far more dominant role in shaping life outcomes than misinformed or racist words that still sting but rarely scar.

The vast chasm between white and black wealth and income serves as a painful reminder of the long road to travel toward racial justice. While too many people are reluctant to acknowledge these realities, they were in plain view during Hurricane Katrina. Yet even the teachable moment of Katrina seems to be slipping from our grasp.

When we look at America and the world at large, we can see vestiges of Jim Crow Jr. rear their ugly head. For instance, less than half of African American and Latinos graduate from high school, compared to 78 percent of whites. The average black family has one tenth the wealth of the average white family. When African American men are incarcerated at more than six times the rate of white men and when black joblessness is more than twice as high as the rate for white Americans, a postracial America represents a mirage.[7] Maternal mortality for blacks is also three times higher than for whites, minority-rich schools are twice as likely to have inexperienced teachers, and blacks' median household income remains at 62 percent of whites', according to a 2010 National Urban League report.[8] In relation to per capita income, African Americans have closed the gap with whites by only three cents on the dollar over the course of nearly four decades. At this rate, it will take over 537 years before income parity is reached. Wealth in the form of savings or home equity serves as a storehouse of economic security. Yet between 1983 and 2004, median black wealth only inched up from 7 percent to 10 percent of median white wealth. At this rate, it will take 634 years to reach equality in terms of household wealth. These statistics paint a stark picture of how profound privileges, opportunities and benefits remain tied to racial difference in America.[9]

Not only is a postracial America disconnected from reality, it subverts the very nature of what we should be striving to achieve. Too often a colorblind society is reduced to one in which people are not discriminated against because of their skin color. Yet this vision and goal falls far short of Dr. King's broader vision of the beloved community, which better approximates God's kingdom ideal in the making. The beloved community is not achieved by erasing the diversity that is often a byproduct of our race and ethnicity, but instead seeks to build a society in which neither punishment nor privilege is viciously tied to racial or ethnic differences, and our diversity becomes respected and celebrated.

In order to move beyond "postracial" we must have a shared vision of the destination we are trying to reach. Without this shared vision and a common destination, we will continue to wander as a nation and, even worse, end up crashing into each other.

A COMMITMENT TO INTERCULTURALISM

The debate around race has been stymied by the lack of a compelling and unifying vision or ideal. For some, we are striving to achieve a colorblind society that no longer sees the distinctions of race. The challenge is that race and ethnicity are proxies for rich cultural differences that shape and influence our identities. The reality is that humanity is neither colorless nor reducible to color. In both positive and negative ways, community is shaped and formed by numerous allegiances tied into our identity. Race, language, culture, ethnicity, nationality, gender, religion, age, sexual orientation and so on mold our worldview, culture and beliefs. We can't and shouldn't be reduced to simply any one of these identities, nor should we have to relinquish them in the pursuit of forming and participating in community. The goal should not be to transcend race, but to transcend the biased meanings associated with race.

In the book *In Living Color*, Emmanuel Lartney outlines a series of approaches to addressing race and ethnicity. These approaches can help us manage and navigate our increasingly diverse and multicultural reality. They include a monocultural, crosscultural, multicultural and intercultural approach. Proponents of the monocultural approach subscribe to a colorblind, culture-free reality based on the belief that "we are all really just the same." The monoculturalist universalizes particular sets of norms, values, cultural beliefs and practices, which at best deny and at worst suppress cultural expressions that do not conform to the mold.[10] When I was growing up, this was often referred to as the melting pot theory. This metaphor has been largely discredited and abandoned because it makes white culture normative and forces people of color to accommodate to this dominant culture.

Crossculturalism recognizes cultural difference and places a high premium on pluralism, holding the view that cultural boundaries are fixed, unalterable and to a degree impenetrable. But this approach reinforces an "us versus them" mentality by overemphasizing difference. The approach is best captured through the metaphor of a salad bowl in which each ethnicity represents a distinct ingredient with its own unique flavor. The danger in this approach is that everything becomes "racial." We start interpreting every action, word and deed through a hypersensitive racial lens.

Multiculturalism is an approach that has been embraced the most within academia. The approach emphasizes that healthy race relations within any community must be based on knowledge and information about the groups constituting the community.[11] Learning about and respecting differences is a critical step toward embracing diversity. However, like crossculturalism, the approach often fails to avoid stereotyping and perpetuating myths within subdominant groups. The approach also lacks an appreciation for the complexity of culture and, at worst, overlooks the reality of individual differences within cultural groups.

Interculturalism combines the best parts of these first three approaches, based on the premise that every person is in some respects like all others, like some others and like no other. Intercultural experience helps us realize that no matter how different culturally or personally people are, there are features of their lives that resemble those of other persons.[12] A sense of shared humanity creates a great deal of common ground for empathy and connection between people in spite of our differences. Our shared humanity binds us together. The fact that we are like some others refers to ways of knowing, interpreting and valuing the world through the socialization we go through in our social groupings. To take persons seriously we must make a genuine effort to tiptoe in their moccasins across the terrain they've traversed. This requires stepping outside our comfort zone and becoming an active listener and learner about cultures that differ from our own. We must remember that different does not mean deficient. People of color are often placed in the unenviable position of speaking on behalf of their entire race or ethnic group, particularly when they are the only African American, Latino, Native American or Asian at their workplace or in the classroom. No matter how many similarities may exist within cultural groups, members within that group are never totally monolithic or homogenous.

The intercultural approach is most akin to a jazz band, in which our God-given diversity represents an incredible strength and asset if properly understood and utilized. Each member of the band plays their own instrument, at times improvising and standing out through a solo, but always coming back to the whole band to generate a tune whose sum is greater than its individual parts.

TRANSCENDING A BROKEN DEBATE

In judging racial progress, psychology professor Richard Eibach found that whites use the yardstick of how far we have come from the nation we used to be, whereas blacks consider how far we have yet to go to become the nation we ought to be.[13] Diverging perspectives on how to measure progress often impact the way we interpret present reality. Alarmingly high rates of joblessness, poverty, lack of educational achievement and incarceration within the black community are often explained as being a byproduct of certain pathologies of reckless or irresponsible behavior. Popular commentators like Bill Cosby have sparked controversy by claiming that African Americans must move out of a constant victim status and take greater responsibility for raising their children, advancing their communities and uplifting themselves through the bedrock values of hard work, prudence and self-respect. While I support the call for greater personal and collective responsibility, this argument often understates the deleterious effects of racial inequality and structural barriers, while ignoring the harmful impact of internalized racism. Calling for greater responsibility without also removing barriers and addressing the effects of internalized oppression becomes hollow and is often ineffective. Different forms of self-negating and self-destructive behavior, whether drug use, crime or promiscuity, are often driven by underlying distress patterns that have become internalized, assaulting people's dignity and suffocating their potential.

The public and political dialogue about race gets stuck in this circular debate between proponents of structural justice versus personal responsibility. In *Race Matters*, Cornel West captured the subtext that underlies our politics, the divide between "liberal structuralists," who focus exclusively on systemic issues like job and residential discrimination, skewed unemployment rates, inadequate health care and poor education, and the "conservative behavioral" camp, who emphasize the waning of a Protestant ethic of hard work, deferred gratification, frugality and responsibility in much of black America. The solution for "structuralists" is the best of President Roosevelt's New Deal and President Johnson's Great Society programs of more government money, better bureaucrats and an active citizenry. Meanwhile "behaviorists" tend to promote self-help programs, black business expansion and nonpreferential job practices.[14]

Like most binary debates, these choices represent a false dichotomy. The real questions are, in which one do we place the greater emphasis? and what is the appropriate and necessary role of government in advancing both structural justice and fostering greater personal responsibility? The structural justice camp is often fearful that any acknowledgment that personal behavior and family breakdown contribute to racial disparities will lead down a slippery slope in which people of color are blamed for their predicament, exonerating the rest of society from taking any responsibility. On the other hand, a refusal on the part of some leaders to acknowledge that the proliferation of single-headed households and breakdowns in the family contribute to social decline lead many moderates and conservatives to tune out and close their eyes to real barriers that block advancement. In a June 15, 2008, speech on fatherhood, then-Senator Barack Obama captured the needed balance between social and personal responsibility, saying "How many in this generation are we willing to lose to poverty or violence or addiction. How many? Yes, we need fewer guns in the hands of people who shouldn't have them. Yes, we need more money for our schools, and more outstanding teachers and more job training and more opportunity in our communities. But we also need families to raise our children. We need fathers to realize their responsibility does not end at conception. We need them to realize that what makes you a man is not your ability to have a child—it's the courage to raise a child."[15] Personal and social responsibility go hand in hand.

Civil society is particularly well situated to promote greater social and personal responsibility and must increasingly step to the plate to instill and reinforce the value of both personal and communal responsibility. This role is particularly true of the church. I commend President Obama's willingness to address sensitive values issues in public speeches and through initiatives like the National Fatherhood Initiative and Let's Move! initiative, the latter focused on reducing childhood obesity. Yet these efforts will stumble and fail without the active participation of religious institutions carrying a great deal of the weight and message. The primary role of government is to create and enforce an equal playing field and to provide a ladder of opportunity for those who have been historically denied access.

RACIAL RECONCILIATION AND JUSTICE

A faith response to racial division and isolation starts with the hard work of reconciliation, which is central to the Christian identity and calling. Reconciliation comes from the Greek word *katalasso*, which means "radical change" or "to change thoroughly from one position to another." According to the Center for Reconciliation at Duke University, reconciliation is God's initiative, seeking "to reconcile to himself all things" through Christ (Colossians 1:20). Reconciliation is grounded in God restoring the world to God's intention; it is the process of restoring the brokenness between people and God, among people, and between people and God's created earth. "Reconciliation between people is a mutual journey, requiring reciprocal participation. It includes a willingness to acknowledge wrongs done, extend forgiveness, and make restorative changes that help build trust so that truth and mercy, justice and peace, dwell together."[16] True reconciliation involves an acknowledgment of past hurts and grievances while avoiding getting stuck in a cycle of blame and recrimination.

The apostle Paul's letter to the Galatians gives Christians a blueprint for pursuing reconciliation in that we "are all sons of God through faith in Christ Jesus, for all of you who were baptized into Christ have clothed yourselves with Christ. There is neither Jew nor Greek, slave nor free, male nor female, for you are all one in Christ Jesus" (Galatians 3:26-28). The Galatians text reminds us that our identity in Christ supersedes other parts of our identity, whether it's our gender, race, ethnicity. Reconciliation is God's exercise of grace toward humans who were created in the image of God. Thus, we are called to adopt God's vision that we are to be members of a diverse and spiritually dynamic family of God.

True reconciliation can't simply stop at forgiveness; it also involves some type of restitution. Racial justice represents a higher bar that requires both removing all forms of discrimination and providing greater access to economic, social and political opportunities. In the post–civil rights era, our legal system and societal norms reject discrimination by race, whether in hiring, purchasing a home, and so on. The much more difficult task lies in reaching consensus around what needs to be done to rectify past wrongs and recognize that the long midnight of racial subjugation shows up in our present-day reality. Rectifying actions can include affirmative action programs, investments targeted at disadvantaged communities and even some form of reparations. Racial reconciliation without a commitment to racial justice is often incomplete.

The experience of the Truth and Reconciliation Commission (TRC) in South Africa illustrates both the power of forgiveness and the tension in pursuing reconciliation without justice. The TRC was a courtlike body in which victims of gross human rights violations were invited to give statements about their experiences, and some were selected for public hearings. Perpetrators of violence could also give testimony and request amnesty from both civil and criminal prosecution. The commission was empowered to grant amnesty to those who committed abuses during the apartheid era, as long as the crimes were politically motivated, proportionate and there was full disclosure by the person seeking amnesty. The commission was founded based on the belief that without uncovering the truth behind the atrocities committed under apartheid, South Africa would be captive to its brutal past. The fact that political leaders, particularly Nelson Mandela, were able and willing to forgive the atrocities committed under apartheid is a testament to their moral courage. The TRC also promised to provide a form of reparations to victims, though this part of the process was poorly defined and inadequately pursued.

A 1998 study by South Africa's Centre for the Study of Violence and Reconciliation and the Khulumani Support Group, which surveyed several hundred victims of human-rights abuse during the apartheid era, found that most people felt the TRC had failed to achieve reconciliation between black and white communities. Most believed that justice was a prerequisite for reconciliation rather than an alternative to it, and that the TRC had been weighted in favor of the perpetrators of abuse. Without seeing tangible improvements in housing, education, jobs and development, to the black majority the TRC represented a lion without teeth. In many respects America has yet to fully take the step of exposing and owning up to its racial past. While we commemorate Dr. King's holiday each year, the focus is too often on what's already been achieved instead of what lies unfinished.

On its own, reconciliation fails to reverse the disparities that still undermine the creation of the beloved community. Disparities are seen most blatantly in the education system. A Civil Rights Project report puts this trend in stark relief, offering sobering evidence that fifty-five years after the pivotal *Brown v. Board of Education* decision, "blacks and Latinos in American schools are more segregated than they have been in more than four decades."[17] According to the report "schools remain highly unequal, sometimes in terms of dollars and very frequently in terms of teachers, curriculum, peer groups, connections with colleges and jobs, and other key aspects of schooling."[18] The report argues that "desegregation plans that were successful for decades are being shut down by order from conservative courts, federal civil rights officials have pressured communities to abandon their voluntary desegregation efforts, and magnet schools are losing their focus on desegregation. . . . Millions of nonwhite students are locked into 'dropout factory' high schools, where huge percentages do not graduate, have little future in the American economy, and almost none are well prepared for college."[19] The consequence is "a system of segregation by race, poverty, and, increasingly, language, in which most black and Latino students never receive similar opportunities, similar peer groups, or any real chance to connect with or learn how to operate comfortably in middle class white institutions and networks."[20] The majority of white students also suffer from this trend, lacking any real preparation for functioning well in "diverse or predominantly nonwhite settings where many of them are destined to work and live in an era in which whites will become a minority in the U.S."[21]

Education has become the civil rights imperative of our time and one of the most critical issues facing our economy. We can no longer afford a quality education to be determined so much by zip code. The Obama administration has made education reform a flagship priority, in part by incentivizing reforms within states and school districts to institute greater pay for performance, more flexible charter schools and greater school choice. These investments and reforms represent a critical starting point. Transforming our education system will also require a great deal of shared sacrifice and commitment.

The criminal justice system represents an incredible source of continued racial injustice. Prisons have become the surrogate father for far too many black men, resulting in what the Children's Defense Fund calls "the cradle to prison pipeline." Thirty-eight percent of prison and jail inmates are African American, compared to their 13 percent share of the overall population. A black male born in 2001 has a 32 percent chance of spending time in prison, while at the same point in his life, a Hispanic man has a 17 percent chance, and a white male has a 6 percent chance. [22]

While there is no magic bullet or panacea for advancing racial justice, a combination of policy changes and targeted investments and interventions are needed to remove barriers, increase access to opportunity and promote greater security for marginalized groups—including greater access to affordable housing, child care, job training, tax credits that reward work, financial management skills, safer neighborhoods and higher-achieving schools.

Advancing racial justice and pursuing reconciliation are inextricably linked in the context of building the beloved community. Without a commitment to both we risk falling into the pattern of blaming the victims of racism and oppression. As was previously noted, personal and community responsibility also play a pivotal role. Yet a call for greater personal responsibility often rings hollow because it fails to address or heal underlying internalized pain. Racism distorts and deforms the image of God within us and becomes internalized in unhealthy and destructive ways, a process called internalized racism.

HEALING INTERNALIZED RACISM

Brilliant rays of sunlight reflected off the faces of a million men standing together in an arc of brotherhood on the U.S. Capitol mall. It was an awe-inspiring sight and an even more poignant feeling standing tall among black men from every corner of the country representing multiple generations. Fathers stood with their sons, pastors with their parishioners, along with both newfound and long-lost friends.

In the fall of 2005 I traveled with a group of students from Emory University to Washington, D.C., for the Million Man March. The march left an indelible imprint on my mind and spirit, teaching me a great deal about the power and importance of overcoming internalized racism. Media controversy over Louis Farrakhan's leadership in convening the march cast an unfortunate shadow over it. While I strongly disagreed with many of Farrakhan's views and statements, the call for greater personal responsibility and empowerment among black men was long overdue. For those who attended, the march was about much more than Farrakhan.

The march got mischaracterized by the media as being primarily a political one when, in reality, I found it to be deeply spiritual call to atone for abandoning and neglecting our duties as black men. It was a call to heal and mend our divisions and to take greater responsibility over our lives. Sometimes we have to take the plank out of our own eye before we can remove the speck in the eyes of others. The march also called for reconciliation between men and their families and communities. Speakers called participants to overcome the divisions and unite to create a productive and supportive environment that fosters in each person the ability to pursue and cultivate the good.

Through an organization on campus called the Brotherhood of Afrocentric Men, I helped to organize a bus for black students from Emory University to attend the march. The road trip from Atlanta to D.C. was like a rite of passage and pilgrimage, a deep bonding experience between thirty black men who were searching and seeking to understand who we are and what our educational achievement requires of us. I distinctly remember the incredible sense of pride, hopefulness and community that we felt on that brilliant day. For one day, black men from every generation came together in a spirit of brotherhood, putting their guard down and revealing their hurts and failures. The day personified unity. But somehow the fervor of that day dissipated far too quickly, as though an ocean of taking greater responsibility receded back into the sea of daily pressures and old habits. I'm sure there were countless ways in which men's lives were transformed by the march that can never be fully quantified, but somehow the march failed to sustain a sense of urgency for greater accountability and responsibility.

The history of racial exclusion and white superiority has left indelible scars in the psyches of many people of color. Overcoming this barrier is inextricably linked to promoting greater personal and communal responsibility, yet it often gets conveniently left out of the equation. While Moses freed the Israelites physically from slavery, Pharaoh still colonized their conscience as they wandered for forty years in the desert in search of the Promised Land. In a similar light, the civil rights movement freed people from overt legal discrimination and political disenfranchisement, yet deep emotional and psychological scars and economic wounds remained. These scars have become internalized and must be rooted out and healed before people can fully embrace and participate wholly in the beloved community. According to Bakari Kitwana, "a generation must come to grips with the damage we do to ourselves in popular culture (rap lyrics and 'hood films) and in everyday life (inadequate parenting, resentment-filled interpersonal relationships, and inferior educational performance), which stands counter to traditional ideas of Blackness."[23]

According to Suzanne Lipsky, every hurt or mistreatment, if not healed, creates some form of a rigid, destructive or ineffective feeling and behavior in the victim of the mistreatment. This distress pattern, when restimulated, will tend to push the victim through a re-enactment of the original distress experience either with someone else in the victim role or, when this is not possible, with the original victim being the object of her/his distress pattern. Internalized racism reproduces distress patterns that show up in many different forms through self-invalidation, self-doubt, isolation, fear, feelings of powerlessness and despair.

The degree of color consciousness within the black community and many other communities of color represents one overt manifestation of internalized racism. Light skin and straight hair are often deemed preferable and beautiful, while kinky hair and black skin are often demeaned and frowned on. Drugs, alcohol and other addictions; compulsive and hurtful sexual behaviors; flashy consumerism; irrational use of money; all kinds of elaborate street rituals and posturing can all be traced to patterns of internalized racism and oppression.[24]

Healing internalized racism requires fierce and resilient love. Mentorship represents one critical way to identify and reverse many of the distress patterns caused by internalized racism. We must create opportunities to celebrate and express pride in our ethnic and racial identities without being exclusive and ethnocentric. Schools and workplaces that affirm and celebrate cultural diversity provide an important antidote, ensuring that people of color don't feel pressured to check their ethnicity at the door or tone down their racial identity. The subtle and overt messages in television, music and media that demean, degrade and dismiss people of color must be increasingly replaced by images and messages that uplift, celebrate and honor their contributions and achievements. The work of uprooting and healing internalized racism will be slow and painstaking, but it is critical for restoring wholeness, reaffirming people's dignity and catalyzing the healing that lays the groundwork for reconciliation.

CHAPTER 9

FROM NARROW NATIONALISM TO GLOBAL LEADERSHIP AND CITIZENSHIP

THE WORLD HAS BECOME MORE INTEGRATED and compressed than ever before—a living parallel to the body that Paul describes so eloquently in 1 Corinthians.

> The body is a unit, though it is made up of many parts; and though all its parts are many, they form one body. So it is with Christ. For we were all baptized by one Spirit into one body—whether Jews or Greeks, slave or free—and we were all given the one Spirit to drink. . . . But God has combined the members of the body and has given greater honor to the parts that lacked it, so that there should be no division in the body, but that its parts should have equal concern for each other. If one part suffers, every part suffers with it; if one part is honored, every part rejoices with it. (1 Corinthians 12:12-13, 24-26)

In this first letter to the church at Corinth, the apostle Paul offers a brilliant and compelling metaphor likening the church to the human body. The Bible tells us that we are fearfully and wonderfully made. One can only marvel at the biological and physiological miracle that constitutes the human body. If the church is meant to function according to the design of the human body, then each part of the body or each member, in the case of the church, becomes indispensable and interdependent. Verses 25-26 say it best: "its parts should have equal concern for each other. If one part suffers, every part suffers with it; if one part is honored, every part rejoices with it." Dr. King captured the essence of this text when he said, "injustice anywhere represents a threat to justice everywhere."

If we were to take to heart the notion that "if one part suffers, every part suffers with it; if one part is honored, every part rejoices with it" (1 Corinthians 12:26), we could begin to understand our interdependence in new and profound ways. The test of our global leadership, and the key to our collective security, is whether we can globalize a commitment to human rights that affirms and protects human dignity and safeguards freedom.

The body of Christ has become an increasingly international one due to the explosive growth of the church in the Global South. The fastest growing churches are not in North America or Europe but in Africa, the Caribbean and Southeast Asia. Today 70 percent of Christians live outside of North America and Europe. In 1900 this number was merely 10 percent. Every second, two more people surrender their lives to Christ somewhere in the world. If you want to visualize a typical Christian today, picture a rural woman living in a village in Nigeria or a young man in a favela or urban slum in Brazil. New converts are proliferating across the Global South, yet a lack of understanding and deep relationship with these new Christians drives an unnecessary wedge between us. Yet the southern church could help save the northern church from its indifference and fragmented faith.

Trillions of dollars are transferred every day through financial markets while goods and services are traded across borders. Social media have made communicating across the globe as easy as setting up an email or Facebook account. The Internet age has generated new tools, methods and opportunities for organizing almost every aspect of our lives. In this rapidly changing and collapsing world we must act and think both locally and globally. Our moral obligations extend beyond simply our local community, neighborhood or locale. In a global body, our civic and consumer decisions have far-reaching implications for people across the world.

GLOBAL CITIZENSHIP

Every two years the Olympic Games provide a vivid reminder of the potential for global cooperation and harmony. It seems fitting that I started writing this manuscript as the 2008 summer Olympic Games were getting underway in Beijing, China, and am now finishing revisions as the 2010 Vancouver games get started. The Olympic opening ceremony provides a fitting backdrop for the concept of global citizenship. The parade of nations represents a kaleidoscope of color and contrast, with athletes from every part of the globe seeking to get a taste of the indomitable Olympic spirit. As athletes seek to achieve personal triumph and bring honor back to their home nation, a powerful camaraderie develops between them based on the common bond as Olympians. Patriotism is counterbalanced with global consciousness and identity. Even deep-seated rivalries and enmity between sworn enemies are often softened and superseded by this Olympic spirit.

In 1996, I had the privilege of being in Atlanta during the Olympic Games. I spent some time in the Olympic Village at the invitation of a friend of mine from high school who competed in the pole vault for his birth country of St. Lucia. Walking through the village felt like a tour of the United Nations, complete with athletes of every nationality, religion and culture blending together to form a new community of athletes. For three weeks, the Olympic flame burns off the edges of our differences, getting to the core of our shared humanity.

Our world increasingly resembles a neighborhood through the power of trade, commerce and technology. Yet as the world shrinks, our sense of citizenship has remained far too static and insulated. Narrow nationalism describes this condition in which an often misplaced patriotism blinds us to our shared humanity, and allegiance to country trumps the recognition that God shows equal concern for the entire world. I feel especially proud and blessed to be an American. Yet I also know that, from a spiritual perspective, my first allegiance is to God and God's kingdom come.

NARROW NATIONALISM—AN AMERICAN PERSPECTIVE

One of the dangers of narrow nationalism from a U.S. perspective is that we can conflate America's purposes with being the same as God's purposes. But America is not a proxy for God. A belief that God favors American leadership devolves into hubris and a form of triumphalism. While our nation has been blessed with material riches, these blessings can't come at the expense of the rest of the world. As Dr. Richard Land, president of the Southern Baptist Convention's Commission on Ethics and Religious Liberty, writes, "Our ultimate allegiance belongs to God. But God is not an American. He may choose to bless America or judge America, but He is not an American. Many Americans worship Him, but He is not an American. And America's purposes are not necessarily God's purposes. We must never presume that America's policies serve God's purposes. The besetting sin of conservatives is to merge God and country as if they are virtually inseparable."[1]

Too often Americans interpret our role in the world through the lens of American exceptionalism, which refers to the belief that the United States occupies an exalted role among the nations of the world in terms of its national credo, historical evolution, political and religious institutions, and unique origins. The roots of this belief are attributed to Alexis de Tocqueville, who claimed that the then-fifty-year-old nation held a special place among nations, because it was a country of immigrants and the first modern democracy. At worst, exceptionalism feeds a belief that we can do no harm and that the rest of the world hates us only because they envy our freedom and our riches. This defensive and reactionary posture may assuage our consciences but ultimately erodes our moral standing and integrity. A large share of the world's distrust and even enmity toward the United States is not the result of an irrational or extremist ideology but a feeling of having been exploited and mistreated. At the very heart of the fight against the real threat of terrorism is a struggle to win the hearts and minds of people around the world, particularly Muslims. When the United States shows a selective commitment toward advancing human rights and places its commercial interests above its moral interests, we give greater ammunition to extremists who exploit these contradictions.

In times of overreaching and overarching American power, we must articulate a new set of values to define our role in the world. American power that comes at the expense of the rest of the world will create an army against itself. Domination is fundamentally different than moral leadership.

September 11 provided a rare opportunity to close the moral distance between the people and nations of this world. The wanton and tragic attack on the World Trade Center and the Pentagon heightened America's sensitivity about its own vulnerability. Yet raw fear and insecurity overpowered notions of our shared fate and interdependence with the rest of the world. While almost the entire world felt a deep sense of compassion and solidarity with the United States after the attack, this goodwill quickly dried up in the aftermath of the preemptive and ill-concerned war in Iraq. The Bush administration tapped into and fueled deep trauma and insecurity in the aftermath of September 11 to justify an overly belligerent response to both perceived and real international threats. Al-Qaeda terrorist cells became the shadowy enemy, requiring an overreaching Patriot Act and a more muscular foreign policy that demonstrated strength through military might. While might can coerce and conquer, it rarely persuades and often foments an army against itself by stoking humiliation and perceived victimization.

A foreign policy based on a commitment to global citizenship places a greater premium on more consistently advancing human rights and freedoms across the world. The National Security Strategy, the principal U.S. national security document, marks diplomacy, development and defense as the three interconnected pillars of security, yet diplomacy and development often get overshadowed and become subordinated to the goal of defense. In place of unilateral military might, for example, the United States should pursue what Gayle Smith calls "sustainable security," based in the understanding that the United States must maintain its moral authority to lead a global effort to overcome threats to our common security.[2] Sustainable security demands a focus on the security of people as well as nation states, "targeting the fundamental freedoms—from want and from fear—that define human dignity." Sustainable security combines a focus on addressing tangible, proximate threats with also championing our global humanity, because it is the right and smart thing to do. The global challenges of climate change, energy insecurity, terrorism, pandemics, the drug trade, food insecurity, and the illegal trafficking of arms, people and money require global cooperation and global solutions.

Winning the war on terror requires winning the hearts and minds of people who distrust and hate us. While a very small percentage may never be converted, the vast majority can be persuaded through our words and deeds, which requires rejecting the myth of redemptive violence. History bears out that violence begets violence, particularly when it is carried out in retaliation or revenge. The criteria of just war provide a critical set of parameters and principles to govern the use of force as a last and never a first resort.

In 2004, I participated in a consultative process called United States in the World, a project led by the Rockefeller Brothers Fund to fashion communications recommendations for promoting a more cooperative, principled and just foreign policy. We drew from cognitive research showing that deeply held views of the world and assumptions about how the world works guide people's thinking and reasoning in largely unconscious and automatic ways. These mental maps are derived from sources such as "personal experience, cultural norms, mainstream news and entertainment, fables and popular sayings, religious beliefs, and ethical values." These frames function as "shortcuts," or familiar points of reference that enable people to process and assign meaning to new information by relating it to something they already know. Thus, people process and interpret information through the pictures, stories and concepts that are already in their heads. Facts and evidence are often not enough to engage, persuade or mobilize an audience, particularly when they contradict these images and narratives in their heads. In order to break out of the pattern and paradigm of narrow nationalism, we need to develop a new frame that is steeped in a commitment to global citizenship, global responsibility and global community.[3]

EMBRACING GLOBAL RESPONSIBILITY

Global responsibility is tied to the biblical mandate, to whom much is given, much will be expected (see Luke 12:48). In other words, God wants us to use our blessings to bless others, rejecting narcissism and hedonism. In embracing responsibility we refuse to scapegoat the "other" or the "outcast" in order to exonerate ourselves from responsibility. The concept of global responsibility, however, presumes that a nation will take responsibility for its role in perpetuating problems like human rights violations and climate change, and act responsibly in the face of global problems as they occur—acting on the root cause of the suffering.

Engaging in a conversation about global responsibility often devolves into an argument about culpability and blame. Those who believe in the goodness of America and feel a sense of pride about our positive role in the world often fall into a defensive posture when confronted with many of the unjust policies and darker deeds the United States has committed—whether from the propping up of oppressive military governments during the Cold War to deposing the democratically elected government in Iran to lending a blind eye to the genocide in Rwanda to grossly unjust agricultural subsidies that hurt poor farmers both in the United States and around the world. On the other hand, those who have felt victimized by America's contradictions or feel that America has inflicted more harm than good can fall into a dangerous trap of ignoring the incredible contributions and noble deeds of America, from enacting the Marshall Plan to eradicating polio to responding to the devastating earthquake in Haiti to providing AIDS treatment to millions of Africans through the President's Emergency Plan For AIDS Relief (PEPFAR). Perhaps all Americans lie somewhere between these two extremes; however, by and large, everyone along the continuum believes in the ideal and promise of America. The challenge is to get both sides out of a cycle of blame and into a commitment to mutual responsibility. We shouldn't deny the wrongs or grievances that the United States has carried out in the name of democracy or capitalism. Yet we don't need to suffer from amnesia; we can correct revisionist history without making a sweeping indictment of America's global leadership. The truth lies somewhere in between, and as Jesus tells us, the truth will set us free.

The human rights community has often lacked a constituency that is vocal and well organized enough to stop causes of genocide and ethnic cleansing in the world. Samantha Power describes this trend in her searing book *A Problem from Hell.* Power chronicles how American policymakers have been reluctant to condemn mass atrocities of genocide or assume leadership in waging an international military intervention to stop them—from Nazi Germany to Cambodia to Bosnia to Rwanda. Despite the world's commitment after the Holocaust of World War II to "never again" allow genocide to take place, this forward-looking, consoling refrain, while "a testament to America's can-do spirit, never grappled with the fact that the country had done nothing, practically or politically, to prepare itself to respond to genocide."[4]

In contrast to the genocide in Rwanda, which took place almost as a flash flood of vicious killing, the genocide in Darfur, Sudan, has taken place in slower motion. The crisis began in the spring of 2003 when two Darfuri rebel movements—the Sudan Liberation Movement (SLM) and Justice and Equality Movement (JEM)—launched attacks against government military installations as part of a campaign to combat longstanding political and economic marginalization of Darfurians. The Sudanese government responded swiftly and brutally to extinguish the insurgency. Through coordinated military raids by government-armed militia (known as the Janjaweed), the Sudanese military targeted ethnic groups from which the rebels received much of their support. Over four hundred villages were completely destroyed and millions of civilians were forced to flee their homes. An immense humanitarian crisis resulted from the mass displacement of these civilians. As a result of the attacks and the deterioration of living conditions, many experts estimate that as many as three hundred thousand people lost their lives between 2003 and 2005.

In September 2004, President George W. Bush declared the crisis in Darfur a genocide, the first time a sitting American president had made such a declaration regarding an ongoing conflict. Despite this declaration and condemnation from across the global community, the violence continued in Darfur as the number of dead and displaced increased considerably. The United Nations–African Union peacekeeping force (UNAMID) in Darfur replaced an underfunded and underequipped African Union peacekeeping mission in January 2008. In 2010, UNAMID remains without the necessary resources to adequately protect the 2.7 million internally displaced people who live in large camps across Darfur. Overall, the UN estimates that roughly 4.7 million people in Darfur (out of a total population of roughly 6 million) are still affected by the conflict.[5] Despite an incredible outpouring of public concern and grassroots pressure, the U.S. response to Darfur has suffered from a combination of political inertia, competing and crosscutting demands on our foreign policy toward Sudan, and a lack of consensus on the best courses of action.

Since the genocide began back in 2003, Rev. Heber Brown has worked to mobilize churches across Maryland to end genocide in Darfur. He has written hundreds of emails, contacted elected officials from the local level to the White House, preached a month's worth of sermons, has had a drawer full of articles published in local media, collected hundreds of petition signatures, led countless "teach-ins" on the issue and even organized a "Baltimore for Darfur" event to raise awareness. In 2007, Brown organized clergy and concerned citizens in Maryland to advocate for divestment legislation designed to pressure the government in Khartoum to cease its genocidal activities, clear the path of return for those displaced by violence and advance human rights for all throughout the country. According to the *Washington Post*, Maryland had more than $200 million invested in fourteen companies that had ties to Sudan. Shortly after testifying on the divestment legislation, along with radio personality/activist Joe Madison and civil rights–era activist Rev. Walter Fauntroy, the Maryland General Assembly voted to pass the Sudan Accountability and Divestment Act. Shortly thereafter, he joined others in successfully petitioning the Baltimore City Council to follow suit.

Heber's creatively maladjusted campaign against genocide embodies a commitment to global citizenship. Global citizenship entails internalizing a commitment to human rights, such as arms control; stopping human trafficking, terrorism and infectious diseases; reforming and strengthening threats; revamping and increasing assistance to eradicate extreme poverty within a generation; reversing global climate change through smart investments in renewable energy, putting a price on carbon and reducing our carbon footprint; leveling the playing field in the international trading system; and thinking and acting both locally and globally in our personal decisions.

CHAPTER 10

FROM SOLELY SERVICE TO CIVIC DISCIPLESHIP

Those who profess to favor freedom and yet deprecate agitation are men who want crops without plowing up the ground; they want rain without thunder and lightning. They want the ocean without the awful roar of its many waters.

This struggle may be a moral one, or it may be a physical one, and it may be both moral and physical, but it must be a struggle. Power concedes nothing without a demand. It never did and it never will. Find out just what any people will quietly submit to and you have found out the exact measure of injustice and wrong which will be imposed upon them, and these will continue till they are resisted with either words or blows, or with both. The limits of tyrants are prescribed by the endurance of those whom they repress.

FREDERICK DOUGLASS, "IF THERE IS NO STRUGGLE,
THERE IS NO PROGRESS"

Cheap grace is the mortal enemy of our church. Our struggle today is for costly grace.

DIETRICH BONHOEFFER, *THE COST OF DISCIPLESHIP*

DISCIPLESHIP AT ITS CORE IS ABOUT spreading the gospel, following God's Word and demonstrating Christ's love, mercy and justice in the world. Service and activism represent flip sides of a two-sided coin called Christian discipleship. Activism needs service in order to stay grounded and remain connected to the needs and interests of people experiencing the brunt of injustice. Service needs activism, because without it, service can lead to dependency, failing to address the root causes of neglect and need. Young people naturally gravitate to service, in part, because the impact is more immediate and visible than through civic engagement and activism.

Fortunately, the tide is shifting toward embracing both. One indicator of this shift is that the 2009 Urbana Student Mission Convention, sponsored by InterVarsity Christian Fellowship, offered an advocacy and poverty track for the first time. The Urbana conference provides a window into a transformation taking place among young Christians across the United States and the world in embracing justice. At Urbana, thirteen hundred young people chose a four-day track focused on poverty with a subset of four hundred participating in advocacy workshops. Rev. Aaron Graham, the former national field organizer at Sojourners, helped to organize an advocacy track working with World Vision, InterVarsity and International Justice Mission. His firsthand impressions are illuminating:

> My overall feeling was that folks in the advocacy track understood the need for systems change beyond just individual response. I still feel like people at most of Urbana approach justice issues primarily through individual and personal change. People speak about injustices, but the response always comes down to "what are you going to do" rather than "what are we going to do."[1]

Urbana is the most recent expression of the Student Volunteer Movement. This student movement, which swept the country in the nineteenth century and mobilized thousands of young people, started voluntary societies to help recruit, support and send missionaries all across the world.

Samuel Mills was one of the first. In 1806 he felt that call as a student at Williams College when he and some fellow students were praying in a field during a thunderstorm. The Haystack Prayer Meeting birthed the missions movement not only among students but also among people of all ages and in Protestant churches of all types. Many of these missionaries soon became activists as they encountered poverty, sickness and injustice. Samuel Mill's heart was broken for the oppression of slaves, so he founded the American Colonization Society in 1817, with the purpose to evangelize the slaves in America, work toward their liberation and then repatriate them to Africa.

From this context, Graham believes the contemporary Urbana missionary movement represents one of the best chances of birthing a new social movement in America today. Movements start when young people are involved and they are willing to lay down their lives. At Urbana 09 there were seventeen thousand young people worshiping in different languages, crying out to the Lord saying, "Here I am, Lord, send me." According to Graham, "these young people are willing to go wherever, do whatever, whenever. History shows us that social movements start when people of privilege make the choice to join with those who are being oppressed in the fight for justice. Today, a whole new generation of young Christians, many of whom come from educated and privileged backgrounds (like many at Urbana), are making that choice to say no to the American dream and yes to God's dream for a better world."[2]

The theme of Urbana 09 was "He Dwelt Among Us." You would often hear speakers and workshop leaders quoting Eugene Peterson's version of John 1:14 (The Message): "The Word became flesh and blood, and moved into the neighborhood." Students were challenged to identify with the needs of the least, the last and the lost. They were challenged to relocate to urban slums, where one-sixth of the world lives. And they were challenged to relocate to urban America where crime and poverty still pervade.

In the advocacy and poverty track,[3] students were challenged to understand advocacy as mission. The organizers didn't want to just talk about advocacy but actually show how to do it. Together they launched the Human Wrong Campaign,[4] which is focused on ending child slavery. Students wore T-shirts to identify with the two million children who are forced into slavery every year. They gathered over three thousand signatures from other students during Urbana to support the Child Protection Compact Act[5] in Congress, a bill designed to help end child slavery. Many of these students planned to organize campaigns back on their campuses.

Graham was struck by the emphasis that Urbana and InterVarsity placed on daily Bible study. Literally the whole morning was spent in Bible study for four straight mornings at Urbana. It started with personally meditating on the Scripture, then doing an inductive Bible study with a group, then going to the main session where the lead Bible expositor broke down the text. Graham contends that it is this dedication to understanding the Word of God and the context in which it was written that allows so many different people to come together around one same mission.

The worship each night was not only ethnically diverse within a United States context but globally diverse. Graham suspects that Urbana 09 must have been 25 percent Asian American, which is truly incredible. It is clear that Urbana understands and is seeking to communicate to this new generation of students that the center of Christianity no longer resides in America and Europe but rather has shifted to the Global South, to places like Africa and Asia where the majority of Christians now live. This trend has incredible implications for how students think about doing missions today.

Students are realizing that the best contribution they can make to the kingdom of God is not necessarily to go relocate to a country that is now more evangelized than their own but rather to use their voices and privileges to help bring justice to those nations. Students increasingly understand that they have been disproportionately blessed and that this blessing comes with a responsibility, a responsibility to use their voices to speak truth to power and to mobilize their own resources on behalf of those less fortunate. The question for students at Urbana was not whether they should care for the poor, but how they should care. How Christians should engage in politics is still a hot topic that students want to explore more. It seems that more and more students would agree that the gospel should influence public life and the political arena, but the question is how much emphasis should be put in that arena.

The fact that Urbana 09 had an advocacy track for the first time ever was historic; whether advocacy is truly understood as integral to mission for all Christians or whether it becomes an optional expression of mission remains to be seen.

OVERCOMING AN AVERSION TO POLITICS

In an effort to live out a more radical faith, we naturally gravitate toward making changes to our lifestyle that reflect kingdom values and toward direct engagement with the dispossessed through service and missions work. This is part of the reason why the new monastic movement, led by authors and activists like Shane Claiborne, is so compelling and popular. I admire Shane's and others' countercultural commitment to live out the gospel in a more authentic and unadulterated fashion, whether by making their own clothes or living in an intentional community within a blighted and impoverished neighborhood in Philadelphia. In many ways, Shane and the Simple Way are a more contemporary version of the early Sojourners community. Except unlike the early Sojourners, most intentional communities today demonstrate a disinterest in and suspicion of politics.

Political engagement too often becomes the stepchild and the weak or missing link in discipleship, partially because of a fear that engagement in politics will naturally corrupt or compromise our faith. It feels easier and more expedient to relocate to a blighted neighborhood, love our neighbors with daily acts of generosity and hospitality, volunteer in a soup kitchen, buy fair trade products or try to live a simpler lifestyle. As Christians, we are called to live out the countercultural impulses of Christ. This includes the commitments listed above; however, in the U.S. context we can't escape the fact that we live and operate in the midst of a market economy and a democratically elected government makes decisions and sets policies that have a profound impact on the very people Christ calls us to pay the closest attention to. The church is charged to lead by example, both through our own stewardship of resources and the ways in which we interact with institutions of power. As we explored in chapter three, God is Lord over every aspect of our lives, including the political and economic. While fasting from voting may feel like a morally pure and conscionable decision, it also demonstrates a privileged mentality, as you are likely to be more shielded from the consequences.

Tension will always exist between the demands of our faith and the demands of politics. The kingdom of God is never fully represented by any of the political choices on the ballot each year. However, we must use our prudential judgment and spiritual discernment to evaluate which candidate most closely reflects our values, is best qualified, and will be most likely to lead positive change. Our democratic system slowly atrophies as the public disengages from politics. Without a well-informed and engaged citizenry, our system lacks necessary checks and balances of accountability. Money has also seeped into our political system in ways that often subvert the common good, putting commercial interests above the common interest.

Too many young people avoid civic engagement because they believe it will be futile or a waste of time. Chris LaTondresse argues that cynicism and an aversion toward politics stems for many

Christians, particularly evangelicals, from bad experiences and poor role models. He says,

> Many of us raised in the evangelical world were implicitly (and sometimes explicitly) taught that, "if you're a Christian, you vote for Republicans." Young evangelicals have grown up watching our parents' generation closely, and we haven't always liked what we've seen: a narrow focus on criminalizing abortion and preventing gay marriage, an easy endorsement of the war in Iraq and the worst of President Bush's interrogation policies, and an uncritical embrace of the most strident forms of American nationalism. We have watched these supposedly "Christian" values being promoted to the frontlines of America's culture wars in the past two decades, and yet it has not diminished the coarseness of our culture, made our families stronger, our communities more moral or our country safer. My generation is increasingly, and rightfully, cynical toward the forms of political expression and social engagement our tribe has chosen to date. It's no surprise that we feel confused, betrayed, and have second thoughts about politics as an effective—or even biblical—means of kingdom expression or as a vehicle for social justice. This cynicism can easily lead to the belief that serious followers of Jesus ought to stay out of the public arena altogether. This kind of thinking is understandable, but it's ultimately misguided.[6]

Disillusionment and cynicism can lead to a dangerous fasting from politics and a replacement of civic engagement with service. Yet, service at its best inspires and deepens a commitment to activism.

SERVICE FOR SOCIAL CHANGE
Reverend Harry Fosdick captures the transformative role that service and activism can play in the context of faith when he wrote,

"Electricity may not come in where it cannot flow through. So the Christian Gospel demands an outlet before it can find an inlet. The failure of many Christians lies at the point of intake; they are estopped from real faith and prayer; they have no vital contact with divine realities. But the disaster of multitudes comes from a cluttered outlet. They do not know the meaning of service."[7] Service is often reduced to isolated acts of charity and goodwill instead of genuine efforts to build long-lasting and transformative relationships. If we take the vocation of service seriously, both the giver's and the recipient's lives will be transformed by the exchange.

In my senior year at Emory University, I became the service chair of my fraternity chapter of Alpha Phi Alpha. A commitment to service was already branded into the DNA of the fraternity, as we were founded around the motto that "first of all, service to all, we shall transcend all." Every week I would organize different service projects and work to rally my brothers to participate, often physically picking them up out of bed and breaking up their precious Saturday morning sleep. We also participated in a weekly mentoring program at a underperforming and struggling middle school in the heart of Atlanta. Other projects ranged from serving food in soup kitchens to tutoring kids and raising money for various causes. The projects forced us out of our Emory University bubble and often brought us face to face with the city's disinherited and disenfranchised. The majority of young people today could tell similar stories in the context of their service work.

Through these and other experiences, I've developed a deep love and respect for service in its many manifestations. The service phenomenon that has gripped Americans of all walks of life and ages represents an incredibly positive trend. However, too many people confuse service with civic activism and glorify service as a sustainable solution. Although service at its best broadens one's understanding and deepens one's commitment to systemic and structural change, service should help individuals and communities develop the tools to acquire basic resources in order to help themselves and meet their immediate needs. Yet the hidden power of service is that it places us in closer proximity to the challenges and injustices faced by people within our communities. The power lies in gaining experiences that alter our perspective, breaking us out of our comfort zones and bringing us into closer relationship with the "other" in our communities and world.

As we've previously explored, young people have become a service generation, often substituting service for civic engagement. This trend is, in part, because we would rather see the results of our actions than put our trust in the mechanisms of government. Yet our service often misses a critical dimension of interrogation and reflection. While this often takes place informally over meals or during car rides to and from a project, young people often lack the analytical and reflective tools to uncover and address the systemic issues embedded within their experience. In other words, we need to more formally ask the question *why?* in the context of trying to address needs. Service-training curricula have started to close this gap, but these curricula rarely address the political and economic dimensions of need. Without this insight and new analytical tools, service becomes apolitical and divorced from greater civic engagement. The mass media has stamped an image of eighteen- to thirty-four-year-olds as being slackers, overgrown children and procrastinators, as though we're intentionally dragging our heels to avoid reaching adulthood.[8] The common thread joining all members of this generation is a sense of permanent impermanence. It's hard to commit to a family, a community, a job or a path when you don't know if you'll be able to make a living, make a marriage last or live free of debt.[9] We are more likely than our parents' generation to be obsessed with our careers and getting rich quick. For us, achieving wealth, by any means necessary, is more important than anything else, hence our obsession with the materialistic and consumer trappings of financial success.

In order to get to the heart of service and activism, we must develop a deeper sense of calling. Too often calling gets overshadowed and crowded out by the economics and social pressures that young people encounter. Most students graduating from either college or any graduate program face a debilitating mountain of debt. The book *Generation Debt* chronicles these trends in shocking detail. College tuition has grown faster than inflation for three decades, and faster than family income for the past fifteen years, while federal aid has lagged behind. In 1976, the maximum Pell grant covered 72 percent of costs at the average four-year public school, but in 2004 it paid just 36 percent of a much bigger bill. Two-thirds of four-year students are graduating with loan debt, an average of up to $23,000 in 2004 and growing every year.[10] For the almost one in three Americans in their twenties who is a college dropout, prospects for civic engagement and service are even more constrained. Young people are also running a rat race of debt accumulated from credit cards: 76 percent of students overall and 91 percent of final-year students had at least one credit card in 2004.[11] While more must be done, President Obama's 2011 proposed budget takes a significant step forward in offsetting the escalating costs of higher education by proposing a 35 billion dollar increase in the Pell Grant program to benefit low- and moderate-income families.

CIVIC ENGAGEMENT 2.0
Onleilove Alston, a gifted organizer and seminary student at Union Theological Seminary, believes that a younger generation desperately wants a cause to fight for:

> We look at WWII, the civil rights and women's liberation movements, and we want a cause to get behind, we want more than what we have been sold—consumerism. I see more evangelicals engaging in social justice and not being marginalized because of it. When I was in college between

2000 and 2004 it was taboo to be an evangelical fighting for justice, so you had two lives, your faith community and your social justice work. Now I see young evangelicals not having to make that choice because they know that it is possible to do both. I think the biggest barrier blocking my generation from engaging in justice is the feeling that we all need to be a Rev. Dr. King or Gandhi, and thinking that we need to take huge actions instead of seeing that we all have an important role to play. I think the time of one charismatic leader is over. We are in the time of collective leadership. My generation needs a clear goal to fight for and the encouragement to be the change they wish to see in the world.[12]

Whether the cause is environmental justice, fighting poverty and disease, or ending human trafficking, transformed nonconformists must constantly adapt to their changing political and economic environments. This requires inventing new ways to continually make activism appealing, engaging and effective. We must also be personally refreshed and renewed; otherwise, we face the risk of early burnout and fatigue.

Creative maladjustment requires a greater capacity to build consensus, develop teams of leaders and forge common ground. According to Tyler Wigg-Stevenson,

the broadening of the evangelical agenda is because of a coming of age among a generation that didn't live through the culture wars of the 1960s. Younger generations are much more of a blank slate for engaging in social justice with many more options. People are more interested in networks than in institutions and respond more to a flattened leadership structure. American ventures into social justice must at some point involve the democratic process. But our generation lacks an understanding of the democratic process. We are still locked in the 60s protest model for change. Our generation is dominated by a punier moral imagination than previous generations.[13]

Many organizations still favor a more top-down movement building model in which decisions are made at the top and pushed out for broader consumption. This model is anathema to most young people today, in part because the Internet has democratized access to information in ways that can empower local leaders to implement campaigns and programs that are tailored to fit their local context.

Rev. Heber Brown echoes Tyler's sentiment, arguing "my generation's engagement in social justice activism is pioneering. With great ingenuity, we are giving new definition to what it means to be a social justice activist. It's not just marching or picket lines anymore. We've broadened the scope to include technological tools that literally allow us to take action on a number of fronts while sitting at a computer or texting on a cell phone." However, Heber also believes that "one of the barriers blocking segments of my generation from civic engagement is an education system that can't keep up with the latest developments of how we live today. It's not just the absence of technology in far too many American public schools, it's also the curriculum that is not faithful to the diversity of the American experience and does not engender a sense of global citizenship and responsibility. Couple that with an educational pedagogy that views students as 'empty containers' who are tested on how well they can retain and regurgitate stats, facts and figures, and you have a recipe for a disinterested and disconnected youth populace who become devastatingly convinced by the illusion of their futility."[14] The twenty-four-hour media cycle of constant punditry and ideologically biased news also often stifles civic engagement. Fewer and fewer information sources can be trusted as balanced or largely impartial. Instead, we are spoon-fed slanted stories that appeal to emotion and reinforce a preexisting worldview or ideology.

Leslie Tune points out both the power and limitations of new technology, arguing that "blogs, viral emails and petitions, Facebook, Twitter, etc., are critical for getting results but don't help build community in the same way as marches, sit-ins and meetings in the church's basement. We are able to get attention and are considered a voting bloc but I'm not sure that we are closer to having the communities we want to live in."[15] I agree with Leslie that social networking and online advocacy tools are not a substitute for other more traditional forms of organizing, but they can instead enhance and broaden these vehicles.

New wineskins that build on methods of the past are necessary, but they should not be limited to these old and sometimes outdated models. We must tap into people's current reality, unlock their moral imagination and unleash a sense of their own agency to impact their communities and world. The currency of democratic change today is measured in part by persistent and regular contact with policymakers through letters, phone calls, emails and meetings. While these inputs can have diminishing returns, they become one very important barometer for gauging public opinion on any given issue. For instance, during the very contentious debate around immigration reform in 2006, congressional offices were receiving ten times as many calls from opponents of reform legislation than from proponents. Anger and fear often represent a powerful motivating force in politics, generating a surge of pressure that can overwhelm an elected official. Yet the force of hope is even stronger when harnessed and mobilized in the right way.

One concrete example of a successful campaign engaging young people with new wineskins is the 2001 campaign of the Boston-area Youth Organizing Project (BYOP). Teenagers from congregations and schools from across Boston partnered with the Greater Boston Interfaith Organization to address the dire shortage of up-to-date textbooks in Boston public schools. Yoojin Lee remembers youth leaders emceeing an "action" at Roxbury Presbyterian

Church, which was filled with over four hundred youth and adult community members. The eleven Boston City Council members present were asked to make commitments to veto the mayor's budget until it included additional money for textbooks. That fall, a million dollars' worth of new textbooks were delivered as a result of youth and community power.

Aaron Graham, Brian Swarts and Adam Phillips express a valid caution that social justice will become a "fad" for our generation without a necessary staying power. Adam Phillips believes that "we too easily settle for the quick fix, or the idea that certain social justice causes, from creation care to extreme poverty to racial reconciliation to immigration and even human sexuality will be solved quickly without digging in for the long haul to achieve systemic change. Radical change requires not only a commitment to reflection, training, building partnerships and solidarity but also the willingness to embrace sacrificial living. Taking up one's cross and following Christ is about much more than wearing a T-shirt and being on an email list."[16] Brian Swarts echoes that for Generation X,

> Social justice causes, from supporting fair trade to stopping genocide, are no longer part of some radical political agenda, but are ways for us to both do good and feel good about ourselves. Rather than dreaming of traveling the world on a yacht or clubbing in Amsterdam, we want to dig wells in Rwanda or promote peace in Palestine. Many who would have become bankers or Silicon Valley giants are now becoming "social entrepreneurs"—measuring success in social change rather than stock prices. In many ways social justice has become "hip" and everyone wants to find their cause. But, of course, this has its shortcomings. When social justice becomes a trend it loses its countercultural truth. Our movements begin to conform rather than transform the cultures

that we live in. We run the danger of making very big news about very little change. The challenge that our generation faces is that we must be ready to move beyond our initial "infatuation" with social justice and begin to form a mature, lifelong commitment to working for lasting change. We must continue to inject creativity and cleverness, and even coolness, into the work of justice. But we must also have roots deep enough to stay grounded when things get rough.[17]

Aaron Graham reinforces this concern:

I'm very excited that Bono, Angelina Jolie and Brad Pitt are committed to social justice and are raising a lot of awareness about the needs of the world. We need the celebrities to do their part, along with business leaders and elected officials. But what happens when doing the work of social justice is not cool? Will the church still be on the front lines? We are called to do this work in season and out of season. My concern is that in the midst of a consumer-oriented culture and church, we are not raising up Christian disciples that will have the fortitude to persevere when times get tough.[18]

While there are times in which creative maladjustment will reach a tipping point and become cool or mainstream, far more often it encounters resistance and causes friction. Celebrities can play a central role in amplifying and popularizing a cause, but ultimately they can't replace the need for a groundswell of determined activists who are committed to a cause in and out of season.

Andrew Wilkes points to a number of phenomena that shape social justice for a younger generation.

On the one hand, there is the depoliticization of Christians through groups like the new monastics, who are involved in socially uplifting efforts of private healthcare delivery, job readiness, etc., but they possess a bewildering neglect of political issues (beyond social critique) that stunts the political maturity of many young, particularly white, Christians. Then, there is the work of groups like the Hip-Hop Caucus and other youth groups that work on environmental issues and voter registration among overlooked constituencies. . . . The biggest barrier prior to Obama was a lot of cynicism about the effectiveness of politics in creating social change. Some of that cynicism is eroding, but it is still a big issue. Another barrier is the overemphasis on voter registration and voter education. Both are important, but to focus only on these makes people think democracy is only about elections. Perhaps the return of citizenship training on a large scale— something like what SNCC, Operation PUSH and the NAACP used to do—is needed.[19]

One concrete example of applying new wineskins was the 2002 Student Global AIDS Campaign (SGAC) and Health GAP campaign to convince the Coca-Cola Company to extend AIDS treatment to its entire workforce in sub-Saharan Africa. With a great deal of fanfare, Coke made a bold announcement at the 2001 United Nations Special Session on HIV/AIDS that they were going to provide treatment to their entire workforce in Africa. However, the fine print of the promise disclosed plans to cover only 2 percent of their workforce (mostly managers), not the contracted bottlers and distributors who composed the vast majority of their workforce in Africa. While offering AIDS treatment can reduce employee turnover and associated costs, sometimes it is cheaper to abandon and replace low-wage, low-skill workers who get sick than to provide medical care for them.

We were outraged by Coke's duplicity and saw an opportunity to set an ambitious precedent for other major transnational corporations to provide treatment to their workforces. We designed what resembled a David-and-Goliath campaign to convice Coca-Cola to do the right thing by covering the entire workforce.

On September 26, 2002, the Coca-Cola Africa Foundation re-vamped their initiative. The Foundation and three partners (Glaxo-SmithKline, PharmAccess International and Population Services International) announced a commitment to working with Coca-Cola's forty bottlers in Africa to help them expand their health coverage to include HIV infection and antiretroviral drug treatment. The program was estimated to cost the Coca-Cola Africa Foundation four to five million dollars per year. According to Coca-Cola Africa, a total of 44 percent of bottler employees "had agreed to this program or were on existing programs that covered prevention and awareness and treatment," as of October 14, 2002.[20] While we acknowledged that this program was an important step forward, the new program failed to cover children or other dependents, it contained an overly onerous cost-sharing requirement between bottlers and workers, and it was being rolled out too slowly.

In our research phase of the campaign, we recognized that while Coke possesses an incredibly well-known and respectable brand, marketing and name recognition are extremely important to their brand's success. Coke's Achilles' heel is their image, which is particularly important for a growing segment of their clientele—college students. Many college campuses had entered into exclusive contracts with Coca-Cola, including a number of schools within the SGAC chapter network.

We devised a campaign to take advantage of their public-relations sensitivity, mobilizing students at twelve campuses to "kick Coke off their campus" unless Coke expanded and accelerated their AIDS treatment program. The campaign consisted of postcards calling for the company to cover its entire workforce in Africa, directed at Coke's CEO. Students tabled at their major thoroughfares on their college campuses to raise awareness and organized rallies to garner media interest. A couple of campuses in Altanta, including Emory University and Morehouse College, received a great deal of attention because of their close philanthropic ties to Coke. Within a few months, Coke announced changes to their program, in part due to the increased public attention and pressure. Not a single campus was successful in actually kicking Coke off their campus; however, even the threat generated significant leverage due to a great deal of local and regional media attention. Since 2002, the Coca-Cola Company has worked with its independent bottling partners to provide a comprehensive, continent-wide HIV/AIDS prevention and treatment program for the more than sixty thousand Coca-Cola system associates in Africa, their spouses and their children. The program is the largest single program of its kind in Africa, combining prevention, awareness and treatment, including free condoms and confidential, voluntary counseling and testing for associates and their dependents. Antiretroviral drugs are also made freely available to all who need them.

Postcards, media stunts, targeted emails, and creative and compelling education worked to accelerate the timetable of a powerful multinational corporation. Similar to the biblical David, we identified Coke's weakness and capitalized on the unique stones, or resources, that students possessed. The campaign turned upside down the prevalent notion that activism is futile and that a younger generation can't overcome the tranquilizing effects of cynicism and apathy.

Embracing the biblical call to social justice requires embracing greater degrees of civic engagement and involvement. The health and vibrancy of democracy depends on an engaged citizenry, and our obedience to the Word of God and our faithfulness to Christ depend on it. When people stop participating in their government, democracy can easily slip into an oligarchy or autocracy.

CONCLUSION
A LIFETIME SOJOURN

Come to me, all you who are weary and burdened, and I will give you rest. Take my yoke upon you and learn from me, for I am gentle and humble in heart, and you will find rest for your souls.

MATTHEW 11:28-29

That day when evening came, he said to his disciples, "Let us go over to the other side." Leaving the crowd behind, they took him along, just as he was, in the boat. There were also other boats with him. A furious squall came up, and the waves broke over the boat, so that it was nearly swamped. Jesus was in the stern, sleeping on a cushion. The disciples woke him and said to him, "Teacher, don't you care if we drown?"

He got up, rebuked the wind and said to the waves, "Quiet! Be still!" Then the wind died down and it was completely calm. He said to his disciples, "Why are you so afraid? Do you still have no faith?" They were terrified and asked each other, "Who is this? Even the wind and the waves obey him!"

MARK 4:35-41

IT SEEMS FITTING THAT I'M WRITING a conclusion while sitting on my Chuckanut rock, one of my favorite places in the world. My family used to spend major parts of our summers at a cabin on Chuckanut Drive in Bellingham, Washington, a place I associate with a deep sense of inner calm and stunning beauty. On this rocky beach directly below the cabin rests an oversized rock that I affectionately call "my thinking rock." The rock juts out into the bay forming almost a perfect, natural dock and resting place. Repetitive waves hitting the rock generate a rhythmic and soothing sound that enlivens my soul and brings serenity to my mind as I become enveloped in the rock's rugged arms. I'm sharing these details because where I'm sitting has a lot to do with how transformed nonconformists nourish their souls.

Ephesians 6:12 reminds us "our struggle is not against flesh and blood but against the rulers, against the authorities, against the powers of this dark world and against the spiritual forces of evil in the heavenly realms." Injustice, inequality and oppression are driven by spiritual forces that can take their toll on even the most centered and strong-willed transformed nonconformist. Each of us must find a place where our mind, body and spirit can truly be at rest. I just wish mine was a little closer to my home in Washington, D.C. Fortunately, I've discovered a temporary substitute. Another ritual that keeps me centered is taking a run every weekend in Rock Creek Park. The trail winds along a beautiful creek, where I always pause at a set of rocks that jut out into a stream, almost a miniature version of my Chuckanut rock. The adrenaline rush of running frees my mind and calms whatever tumult exists on the inside. God never intended for a gospel of wholeness to be delivered by messengers who are drowning in their brokenness.[2] The back of the boat is that place where we may go to remember who and whose we are. We spend too much time emptying ourselves and not enough being filled up. Activism can be filled with a great deal of pressure, excitement, anxiety and adrenaline that quickly becomes addicting without the proper safeguards. We can lose the ability to be still and simply be present because of the urgency and burden we feel to address injustice. The Hebrew understanding of peace includes wholeness and well-being. Peace is not merely the absence of conflict, but the presence of godly serenity, the presence of God. Thus transformed nonconformists need to create more space to think more deeply, listen more carefully and see more clearly. The goal of our work is to be a co-celebrant and co-creator with God, not to replace God in the work of kingdom building. Spiritual stillness is about daring the silence, standing up to it and remaining within it long enough to experience God differently, if not more deeply.

In surveying over fifteen dynamic, transformed nonconformists between the ages of twenty-five and forty, I discovered how important it was for each of them to adhere to a set of spiritual disciplines and rituals that sustain their engagement in social justice ministry and activism. A number of common threads surfaced, including the importance of prayer, devotions, recreation, community and worship.

PRAYER

Aaron Graham believes that prayer must be a constant discipline. He says: "I pray as I'm walking to and from work. I pray when I'm on the airplane. I pray when I'm driving and when I'm falling asleep. I pray when I'm feeding my baby his bottle. I try to keep a regular journal where I write down my thoughts and prayers. This helps me be reflective and remember to be grateful in the midst of striving ahead for the next thing. Too often we limit God by limiting the times and ways in which we pray."

Rev. Marlon Millner grew up participating in a form of prayer called "tarrying." Tarrying services were particular prayer services where "seekers" sought the power of the Holy Spirit, typically manifested by speaking in other tongues. The prayer, common in traditional Pentecostal churches, is rythmic, repetitive, responsive, focused and physically exhausting. Sometimes Marlon needs these emotionally outpouring forms of prayer. According to Marlon, praise, lament, despair, hope—they are all a part of the circle. These emotionally deep periods of prayer are times where Marlon empties himself and waits for that still, small voice to speak. Alternatively, one can break free emotionally in response to hearing a still, small voice, and at that point the prayer becomes more celebratory than somber. So praying as "seeking the Lord" is important.

Rev. Heber Brown feels that prayer is primary in sustaining his faith-based social justice work. His best prayer encounters are done early in the morning while walking a mile or two. He hears God better before the "noise" of his daily life has begun. Similarly, Yoojin describes how early on in her community organizing work, she discovered a pressing need for silence. She felt that God led her to a local Episcopalian monastery, where an order of monks (the Society of St. John the Evangelist) invited the public to join them in daily worship and on retreats. For the last nine years, she has participated in worship, usually several times a week, and has made retreats at least every six months or so. She has learned a great deal from witnessing the way these monks try to live intimately with and wholly dedicated to God. In addition, her personal prayer life is as central and necessary as breathing. She has learned different forms of prayer and meditation. Anthony DeMello's book *Sadhana* has been especially helpful. Each morning, she tries to spend some time in prayer.

Finally, Brian Swarts says that "while I can't claim to spend four hours a day in prayer, for me prayer is how I stay connected to the source of my inspiration and strength in this work—to God and his work of redemption. Without prayer, I lose my way."

COMMUNITY

Aaron Graham captured the importance and evolving notion of community in saying, "Twittering, Facebook, and hanging out in big groups is not community for me. I have to be going deep with people so that they really know my struggles and I know theirs. This happens in our church community, in our small group, with the guests that come and visit us, and with a group of my college friends." According to Adam Phillips, "intentional friendships of accountability and practice are critical." Brian Swarts calls "community an essential spiritual discipline. It may seem funny to call this a discipline, but working with other people can be difficult and messy and it means making sacrifices of our time and independence. Yet, at the heart of injustice are broken relationships, and the only way to mend broken relationships is to build community. These communities become both means and ends for our work."

Tyler Wiggs-Stevenson believes that being a faithful member of his local church is imperative to keeping himself humble and grounded. His participation reminds him of purposes and aims at the local level, helping him avoid getting distracted by the national level. He would lose his moorings if he thought he was operating in too large a sphere to not be involved in a local church. This means, for example, going to Sunday school and serving on the missions board. Yoojin, an active member of Cambridge Community Fellowship Church, needs this congregation where they support each other in a collective pursuit of social justice and racial reconciliation. She meets with a smaller group of believers on a regular basis to share and pray with one another. Being in active and accountable relationships with a body of believers helps her grow and protects her from the vulnerabilities of isolation and temptation.

Josef says that most important is time with family, away from work. This time reaffirms the purpose of the work and reminds him of the limits of what he can or cannot do, that "I and the work I do are not the same thing." Being a dad to his son and a husband and partner to his wife is as important, if not more so, as any social justice initiative or issue he might work on. Strong and deep family relationships thus become ground zero for shaping and grounding our creative maladjustment.

RESPONDING TO THE *KAIROS* MOMENTS

South Africa has taught me a great deal about *kairos* moments. Chronos represents the normal, inexorable passage of time. Meanwhile, *kairos* represents time through God's watch. There are Spirit-filled moments in time in which normal time is replaced by new possibilities and opportunities because the Spirit is hyperactive. We can never know the exact time and place when this happens, but we can be sure that God knows. I believe that the fall of the Berlin Wall, the March on Washington and the abolition of slavery are all examples of *kairos* moments in which God moved through bold and courageous transformed, nonconformed leadership. South Africans taught me that *kairos* moments respond to the acute signs of the times, when the circumstances around us become so perverted and fraudulent that incremental reform and gradual change are not enough. We may never be able to fully know when we are in the midst of a *kairos* moment. However, we are called to constantly and diligently prepare for the *kairos* moment, knowing that God can work miracles through leaders who are willing to be transformed and refuse to conform to notions of what's considered possible or the status quo.

OVERCOMING THE ACTIVIST TEMPTATIONS

Transformed nonconformists must resist and overcome the temptation and dangers of being defined exclusively by our activism. When our identity is based entirely in what we do rather than in who we are, we enter treacherous territory. In an externally driven state of identity, life is fragile, vulnerable and at risk. Criticism, adversity or failure can shatter that identity far too quickly.

Our involvement in social movements and identity as a transformed nonconformist can be an ego-enlarging and heady enterprise. Over time, activism can become as much about us as it is about the people whose lives we are trying to touch and transform. Success and fame can often take our ego to places that our integrity and character cannot fully sustain. That's why it is critical to put in place certain checks and balances. No matter how influential our voices might become, ultimately everything we do is to God's glory and to advance God's kingdom. Activism should not solely define us. The great jazz musician Miles Davis said, "I am not what I do, I do what I am." This simple but poignant quote points to the danger of allowing our entire identity to become wrapped up in our pursuit of social and political change. The risk increases when we step out of a particular leadership role or some kind of misfortune takes away the attention, responsibility and accolades that we so often thrive on.

I've learned the hard way the lies of invincibility and indispensability that so often haunt the lives and livelihoods of transformed nonconformists. Rev. Kirk Byron Jones speaks in great detail about these dangers in his book *Rest in the Storm*. While the book is written for ministers, the forewarning and advice is relevant to everyone. Transformed nonconformists overdose on overcommitment and often experience the violence of overload. As a part of our work we must accept and learn to love the humanity in ourselves, which includes embracing our limitations. For me this has required confessing the deleterious effects of excessive activity and learning when and how to say no.

The other danger is that we become defined by what we are against, always assuming a posture of resistance and being in a perpetual state of indignation. As a result, we can also grow bitter and resentful toward those that are in power and start to develop enmity and greater cynicism. This mentality takes a toll and makes our cause or campaigns feel much less magnetic and appealing. Activism at its best should be enjoyable and gratifying, particularly when steeped in the fellowship that comes with greater community built through relationships.

As we engage in activism we must remember Dr. King's forewarning that our means and ends must always be consistent with each other. This requires a "shift from valuing efficacy to valuing faithfulness. According to Tyler Wigg-Stevenson, this approach is counterintuitive unless you believe in the sovereignty of God." Faith has given Tyler a greater sense of how holistic the work of justice needs to be. In other words, you shouldn't have a horrible family life while fighting for justice. Often activists can take out their anger toward injustice on the people closest to them. The kind of just world we are seeking to build starts at home and in our workplaces and should reverberate from the places that are nearest to our lives. This is much easier said than done but is critical to upholding the integrity of our witness and to avoiding cognitive dissonance between our public and private lives.

Finally, contemplation and action are not independent realms. Prayer and contemplation prepare us for action. Not only does prayer give us greater strength and courage, it orders our steps and helps guide our decisions. Howard Thurman's writings have served as an invaluable resource in strengthening my meditative life. Thurman served as the first pastor of an intentionally interracial church in San Francisco. His book *Jesus and the Disinherited* should be required reading for any transformed nonconformist, along with the book *Meditations of the Heart*. Thurman is more of a mystic than a theologian. His words penetrate the soul and offer timeless wisdom. A small taste of what Thurman offers comes through in a devotion titled "How Good to Center Down":

> How good it is to center down!
> To sit quietly and see one's self pass by!
> The streets of our minds seethe with endless traffic;
> Our spirits resound with clashings, with noisy silences,
> While something deep within hungers and thirsts for the still
>   moment and the resting lull.
> With full intensity we seek, ere the quiet passes, a fresh sense
>   of order in our living;

A direction, a strong sure purpose that will structure our
confusion and bring meaning in our chaos.

We look at ourselves in this waiting moment—the kind of
people we are.

The questions persist: what are we doing with our lives? what
are the motives that order our days?

What is the end of our doings? Where are we trying to go?

Where do we put the emphasis and where are our values
focused?

For what end do we make sacrifices? Where is my treasure
and what do I love most in life?

What do I hate most in life and to what am I true?

Over and over questions beat in upon the waiting moment.

As we listen, floating up through all the jangling echoes of
our turbulence, there is a sound of another kind—

A deeper note which only the stillness of the heart makes
clear.

It moves directly to the core of our being. Our questions are
answered.

Our spirits refreshed, and we move back into the traffic of
our daily round.

With the peace of the Eternal in our step.

How good it is to center down![1]

Centering down requires finding those moments to rejuvenate,
replenish and put things in their proper perspective. The beauty is
that we can find very different ways to center down. Try some of
the ones suggested in this chapter. What's most important is that
you make centering down a sacred commitment.

SOJOURNING TOWARD JUSTICE

As was previously explored, transformed nonconformism is about
much more than civic engagement and systemic change. It is directly
linked to a whole series of lifestyle choices and decisions. Living out

a "kingdom lifestyle" helps us transcend the polarizing and often divisive nature of politics. While we must continue to make advocacy and political engagement the central part of our transformed nonconformism, a broader set of lifestyle choices and daily commitments represents critical sources of sustenance and inspiration. Christa Mazone Palmberg touched on this theme, pointing out that

> many in our generation are good at thinking about their politics and faith but aren't always willing to go deep and give of their time and energy. Our generation is so busy that there's an obliviousness to activism because of competing distractions. Dinner parties, social functions, having a family become primary and we become satisfied with too little. Many people lack the tools and resources to get involved. Therefore we need to integrate spiritual formation into social justice work. Social justice is not just about who you vote for but how you spend your money, who your friends are, how you shop, how you spend your time, where your priorities lie in relation to God versus country, etc.

Social justice becomes a "sojourn" or a spiritual journey toward God's kingdom come. While we may take this "sojourn" differently through our respective denominations and Christian faith traditions, we are united by a shared commitment to be "in but not of this world," acting out our faith in ways that transform our communities and the world. Kingdom-lifestyle commitments include praying for justice, making more ethical consumer choices, being better stewards of the earth, participating in service with the disinherited and, of course, political advocacy for systemic change. Being good and responsible parents, supporting healthy marriages, mentoring and caring for children in our neighborhoods are also all signs of transformed nonconformism.

Rev. Heber Brown captures the foundational role that faith plays in fueling activism, sharing that "at different points in my journey, electoral politics has been my starting point. At other times grass-roots revolutionary logic has been the eye of my social justice activity. However, it's been my experience that starting anywhere other than at a place of faith eventually leads me to frustration, depletion and, sometimes, alienation. My process of growth in this area is leading me to deeply value how my connection with Christ represents my source and strength, which positions me to be divinely ordered and sustained. No longer must I rely on my own strength and understanding. I've found unspeakable blessing in depending on God even as a social justice activist. It gives greater meaning to the teaching of Christ that says, 'Blessed are those who hunger and thirst for righteousness; for they will be satisfied'" (Matthew 5:6).

Transformed nonconformists must learn to keep their work in perspective and not take themselves too seriously. While we are co-creators and co-celebrants with God in this kingdom-building project, we must always remember that ultimately our vision and strength comes from the Lord. We can quickly and easily replace God with our own feeble strength and limited vision. One of my favorite gospel songs is "This Battle Is Not Yours, It's the Lord's" by Yolanda Adams. I constantly try to remind myself of this truth. When the battle for a more just world becomes simply my own, I'm prone to greater burn out, disillusionment, exasperation and even fatalism. When I remember and take to heart that the battle is the Lord's, I put my actions in their proper perspective and constantly seek God's Spirit to work in and through me to achieve God's justice in the world.

We must also remember that the ultimate victory is already assured. When we take the long view and remember what Christ has already done on our behalf on Calvary's cross, we know that the fight is already fixed. I once heard Dr. Freddie Haynes offer a captivating sermon illustration of this reality. He said when he was younger he was an avid WWF watcher. Dr. Haynes would be glued to his television as he watched Hulk Hogan annihilate opponent after opponent. No matter how much the odds were stacked against him or how beaten down and broken he looked, Hulk would always find a way to rebound and win the fight. Dr. Haynes abruptly stopped watching when his older brother shattered his reality by convincing him that the fighting that took place in the ring was fake and that ultimately the outcome was fixed. Yet this is the exact mentality that we must have as we engage in transformed nonconformism. Because of Christ's victory over death on the cross, the ultimate outcome is already fixed. Death had Jesus pinned to the floor, but on the third day Christ pushed death aside and rose again. Christ already overcame the sins and injustices of the world on the cross. The in-breaking of God's kingdom of perfect justice, love and peace is already at work in our midst. We are simply called to join God at work in accelerating and spreading the signs of this kingdom come and make them as contagious and irresistible as possible.

As you join or continue the spiritual journey of being a transformed nonconformist, the words often attributed to Oscar Romero provide an indispensable compass along the way. Romero, archbishop of San Salvador, El Salvador, was assassinated on March 24, 1980, while celebrating Mass in a small chapel in a cancer hospital where he lived. He embodied transformed nonconformism through his close relationship to his people, his prophetic preaching of the gospel and his courageous public denouncement of brutal injustice in his country by the paramilitary government. He became the voice of the Salvadoran people when all other channels of expression had been crushed by military repression. Romero said:

> It helps, now and then, to step back and take a long view.
> The kingdom is not only beyond our efforts, it is even beyond
>   our vision.
> We accomplish in our lifetime only a tiny fraction of the

magnificent enterprise that is God's work.

Nothing we do is complete, which is a way of saying that the
Kingdom always lies beyond us.

No statement says all that could be said.

No prayer fully expresses our faith.

No confession brings perfection.

No pastoral visit brings wholeness.

No program accomplishes the Church's mission.

No set of goals and objectives includes everything.

This is what we are about.

We plant the seeds that one day will grow.

We water seeds already planted, knowing that they hold
future promise.

We lay foundations that will need further development.

We provide yeast that produces far beyond our capabilities.

We cannot do everything, and there is a sense of liberation in
realizing that.

This enables us to do something, and to do it very well.

It may be incomplete, but it is a beginning, a step along the
way, an opportunity for the Lord's grace to enter and do
the rest.

We may never see the end results, but that is the difference
between the master builder and the worker.

We are workers, not master builders; ministers, not
messiahs.

We are prophets of a future not our own.[3]

I pray that we get a chance to meet along the way as together we
create a future not our own, serving as God's transformed nonconformists—workers and ministers of a kingdom that continues to
break into our midst but whose full realization is always on the
horizon.

EPILOGUE

When spider webs unite, they can entangle a lion.

ETHIOPIAN PROVERB

IN MARCH 2010, Fox News personality Glenn Beck tried to convince his audience that "social justice" is a "code word" for communism and Nazism. Beck urged Christians to discuss the term with their pastors and to leave their churches if leaders would not reconsider their emphasis on social justice. "I beg you," he said. "Look for the words 'social justice' or 'economic justice' on your church website. If you find it, run as fast as you can. . . . Am I advising people to leave their church? Yes!"

Beck's tirade galvanized a chorus of voices from across the political and theological spectrum, including his own Mormon Church, to reject his outrageous claim. Sojourners launched an email campaign urging Christians to turn themselves in to Glenn Beck for being a proud member of a "social justice" church. Over fifty thousand Christians responded to the call. Beck eventually qualified his statement, conceding that the Bible did call on Christians to help the poor through individual acts of compassion and charity—but not through collective action. The entire episode is a stark reminder of the debate that previously drove a wedge within the church around the role of social justice.

Fortunately, that debate has become increasingly outdated and obsolete, particularly for a younger generation. Christians across the spectrum are embracing the biblical call to seek both justice and righteousness, to pursue evangelism as well as systemic change, to redeem individual lives as well as transform society as a whole. Old dichotomies and false binary choices are becoming vestiges of the past. The Beck debacle provides further evidence that the question is no longer whether Christians should care about and champion social justice but instead "What do we mean by 'social justice,' and how do we go about achieving it?" The challenge facing the church is how to make social justice more than simply an extracurricular activity within the body of Christ but part and parcel to discipleship.

On the day of the inauguration of Barack Obama as the forty-fourth president of the United States, I was with Dr. Vincent Harding, an unsung hero of the civil rights movement and the shadow author behind Dr. Martin Luther King's historic speech "A Time to Break Silence." I shepherded him through an almost impenetrable crowd on the Washingon Mall to see history in the making. One day previous I had been given the honor of introducing him at a program sponsored by Sojourners. As I shared why I felt the impending inauguration represented a watershed moment, my voice began to tremble uncontrollably and tears began streaming down my face. I wasn't speaking from a partisan perspective or as a black man with a biracial background; I was speaking as a person of faith who felt history was being made in our midst, who believed the election represented a poignant turning point for the United States and the world.

Leading into the 2008 election, I decided to apply for the White House Fellowship program. I had heard a great deal about the program over the years from multiple friends; founded by President Lyndon Johnson and supported by every administration since, the White House Fellowship is a nonpartisan program that exposes promising leaders from a diverse range of professional backgrounds to leadership at the highest levels of the federal government. I was granted the fellowship in the summer of 2009.

The year-long fellowship has been a true whirlwind experience, giving me the privilege to meet and learn from a broad range of current and former administration officials, journalists, corporate CEOs and opinion leaders about politics and leadership: almost every member of President Obama's cabinet, journalists David Brooks, Joe Scarborough and Gwen Ifill, General David Petraeus, Illinois Senator Dick Durbin, and District of Columbia public schools chancellor Michelle Rhee, among many others. The fellowship also provided an opportunity to spend an intense year with an extraordinary group of leaders that I've come to admire and love.

I had a feeling that stepping into the inside of government would stretch and challenge my creative maladjustment. One of the dangers of activism is that it is often easier to simply criticize from the outside while lacking sufficient understanding of the constraints and forces that are at work on the inside that make legislating and governing so difficult. Through the fellowship I hoped to become intimately familiar with the range of constraints, competing pressures and institutional barriers that make political change challenging in order to grow into a more savvy and effective advocate. Despite my having earned a master's degree in public policy and spent over ten years in advocacy and organizing, the year has been a steep learning curve in how much I didn't know about the policymaking process.

Reverend Susan Johnson Cook, a former White House fellow during the Clinton administration, served as my mentor. She forewarned that I needed to take care of my soul while I was working in the White House. I quickly realized that she was right; being on the inside of government can erode some of your passion and dampen your sense of the possible. The political realm often requires and rewards expediency and pragmatism rather than conviction and principle, putting a premium on compromise and—more recently—on obstruction, winner-take-all-scenarios, constant campaigning and short-term thinking. The realm of politics, I've learned, is intrinsically different from the realm of faith.

Half the battle serving in government is realizing how often advocates on the outside overestimate what presidential leadership can do to move an agenda, while presidential advisors can sometimes underestimate the power of the president to shift public opinion and galvanize the public. In the midst of these and other obstacles we must learn to be creatively maladjusted even in some of the most compromising and constraining environments—whether it's the corporate boardroom or the corridors of power in Congress. Even if our environment actively discourages our creative maladjustment, we are nourished and sustained by hope.

The dominant fissure in American politics has become the question of the proper role of government. The battle between big and small government, state intervention versus reliance upon the free market, is not a new one. However, this long-standing division has taken on a more shrill, strident and polarizing tenor, most recently manifested in the debate over health care reform and in the tea party movement.

The health care debate revealed much of the brokenness within our political system and our civic culture. Fear and misinformation were used as bludgeons to oppose reform, while many entrenched special interests spent an inordinate amount of money to block reform. The insurance industry alone spent $260 million on lobbying to defeat the bill. Obstructionism became more expedient than genuine efforts to find common ground in Congress.

Imagine if the health care debate had started from the basic value-based premise that every person deserves access to quality health care, mirroring the imperative in Matthew 25. This may seem like an excuse to simply shroud a liberal goal of universal coverage in religious garb. However, there are multiple ways of getting to universal access, and well-intentioned and equally committed Christians can disagree over the best policy path. Yet too often ideological commitments trump spiritual commitments and block common ground.

In writing this book, I tried to resist the cardinal temptation of most preachers—to cram in way too much content. Prayerfully this book won't be my last. Still, I wish I had more time and space to delve into greater detail about a range of policy issues, whether it's the war in Afghanistan, nuclear disarmament, human trafficking, Wall Street reform, immigration, or many others. Instead, I've tried to introduce a set of theological and analytical tools for approaching and addressing these and other complex issues. Most of the issues I've focused on are those closest to my heart and experience; they also often are perceived as being "progressive" causes. I'm committed, among other things, to dramatically reducing the number of abortions in America and fostering healthy marriages; causes like these tend to be associated with a more conservative agenda. The tendency to pigeonhole issues into such overly ideological camps is part of the problem. Regardless of the issue, the basic toolset laid out in this book can be tailored and applied to a range of issues. Unpacking the new methods and strategies that are needed to create social and political change demands a separate book (my shameless plug for a potential sequel). We must continue to learn from one another around what methods and strategies are most effective by sharing our constant reflections about what works, what fails, and why.

I still believe that the faith community possesses the unique power to serve as a desperately needed bridge, buffer and catalyst for change and transformation. The faith community at its best can bridge some of our most immutable divisions, creating a safe space for real deliberation and dialogue; it can serve as a buffer against the ascendance of narrowly conceived naked self-interest, helping us focus instead on the common good; and it can be a catalyst for change, generating urgency and breaking through the inertia of comfort, apathy and convenience.

Ultimately, transformed nonconformism is not simply about up-lifting and empowering others but also about our own liberation and fulfillment. This reality takes us full circle to the prophet's timeless message in Isaiah 58: only after we show compassion to those in need and break chains of injustice will our light shine like a noonday sun. The great preacher Henry Fosdick remixes this no-tion in his book *The Meaning of Service:* "If you wish blessedness, head for service; if you wish the crown of joy, take up the cross of sacrifice; if life is to be yours, lose your life in other lives and in causes that have won your love."

Sacrificial service and collective action represent the dual com-mitments of the transformed nonconformist. I love the image and metaphor of a spider web. Each individual strand is weak and eas-ily breaks. But when tied together, the web forms a durable and powerful force; it can, as the Ethiopian proverb says, "entangle a lion." The world faces lions in many forms—whether global cli-mate change, extreme poverty, an epidemic of violence, modern-day slavery, religious persecution or the HIV/AIDS pandemic. The pressing question remains: Will you join the web of the creatively maladjusted, dedicated to mobilizing hope for their community and world? If not now, then when?

AFTERWORD

MOBILIZING HOPE offers concrete evidence that a younger generation is building on many of the lessons learned from the civil rights movement and applying them to the challenges facing our nation and world today. In the spirit of the Student Nonviolent Coordinating Committee, Adam Taylor has made conscious decisions to get in the way of injustice—whether it's the AIDS pandemic, the pervasive scandal of poverty, or in ending the genocide in Darfur. These choices have caused ripples in the waters of social and political change, defying the stereotype of his generation as being complacent and apathetic. Fighting more covert and institutionalized forms of injustice requires new wineskins, many of which are described in this book. Yet even the most sophisticated tools, strategies and methods fall short without the power of faith. I'm proud to see the struggle to build God's beloved community continue through the creative maladjustment of a committed minority of transformed nonconformists highlighted in these pages. I hope and pray that you will join this growing movement by mobilizing hope and putting your faith into action.

Congressman John Lewis

TRANSFORMED NONCONFORMISTS

IT'S BEEN MY PRIVILEGE, through my work with Sojourners and various other organizations, to get to know and work alongside several young people who fit the description Dr. King offered of "transformed nonconformists"—people who, as Jim Wallis puts it, "creatively apply their faith in fresh, bold and innovative ways." I interviewed a few of them for the purposes of this book; a brief biography of each follows.

Onleilove Alston, a native Brooklynite, met Christ as a teenager and worships him through works of justice. Currently a student at Union Theological Seminary and Columbia University, she organizes with New York Faith & Justice and The Poverty Initiative. As a 2008 Beatitudes Society Fellow, Onleilove interned at Sojourners and is a member of The Special Communion Blogging Collective.

Christa Mazzone Palmberg works as an organizer with Sound Alliance, an organization of diverse religious institutions, education organizations, unions and other civic nonprofits organizing for the common good in Puget Sound. She serves on the board of directors of Sojourners and is an active member of Seattle First Covenant Church.

Marlon Millner is a third-generation pastor in Philadelphia, Pennsylvania, and an elder in the Apostle Church of Christ in God. He is a cofounder of Pentecostals and Charismatics for Peace and Justice, and was elected to town council in Norristown, Pennsylvania. Marlon earned a bachelor's degree from Morehouse College and a master of divinity degree from Harvard Divinity School.

Chris LaTondresse is the founder and executive director of Recovering Evangelical (www.recoveringevangelical.com), an online media portal for next-generation evangelicals, post-evangelicals and those outside the church who still like Jesus. LaTondresse's work has appeared in *Relevant* and *Sojourners,* and been profiled on *ABC News* and *Fox News.*

Andrew Wilkes is a graduate of Hampton University and Princeton Theological Seminary. His vocation is driven by the Micah 6:8 call to "do justice, love mercy, and walk humbly with your God." He is a 2010-2011 Coro Fellow in Public Affairs in New York City.

Aaron Graham serves as the lead pastor of The District Church, a new community of faith located in the heart of Washington, D.C. Before moving to D.C., Aaron started the Quincy Street Missional Church in a low-income neighborhood of Boston, where he served for five years. Most recently Aaron worked as the justice revival director and national field organizer for Sojourners. He is a graduate of Harvard's Kennedy School and is currently pursuing a doctorate at Fuller Theological Seminary. Aaron and his wife, Amy, live in the Columbia Heights neighborhood of D.C. with their son, Elijah.

Brian Swarts has worked as a fourth-grade teacher, faith community organizer, foreign policy analyst and international development practitioner in Africa and Latin America. He is currently the microfinance specialist for the Salvation Army World Service Office and lives in Washington, D.C., with his wife Izumi.

Doug Shipman is currently serving as the executive director of the National Center for Civil and Human Rights. Most recently a principal in the Atlanta office of the Boston Consulting Group, he has worked at various times out of BCG's Atlanta, New York and Mumbai offices with senior executive clients within the financial services, consumer goods and industrial goods industries. Doug has also served as a facilitator for discussion groups exploring racial understanding in Richmond, Virginia, and Cambridge, Massachusetts. He has a master's degree in public policy from the Kennedy School of Government at Harvard University, with an emphasis on domestic politics, and a master's degree in theological studies from the Harvard Divinity School, with an emphasis on religion in public situations and politics.

Rev. Leslie Copeland-Tune is a student at New Brunswick Theological Seminary, where she is working on her doctorate in urban ministry. She has served as assistant director of justice and advocacy for the National Council of the Churches of Christ and continues to serve on the National Council of Churches' Special Commission for the Just Rebuilding of the Gulf Coast. She earned her M.B.A. from the University of Maryland with a concentration in marketing, and a master of theological studies degree from Duke University.

Yoojin Janice Lee's work to support leadership development and political mobilization for social justice stems from her faith. Ms. Lee currently provides training and consulting to coalitions, government agencies and community groups through Health Resources in Action, a Boston-based, public health organization. She was formerly executive director and lead organizer of the Boston-area Youth Organizing Project, where she assisted teenagers from low-income communities of color in building power for justice in their schools and neighborhoods. She graduated from Smith College and holds a master's degree in public policy from Harvard University's Kennedy School of Government. She belongs to the Cambridge Community Fellowship Church and worships regularly with the Society of St. John the Evangelist, an order of Episcopalian monks.

Josef Sorett is an interdisciplinary historian of religion in America, with a particular focus on black communities and cultures in the United States. His research and teaching interests include American religious history; African American religions; hip hop, popular culture and the arts; gender and sexuality; and the role of religion in public life. Josef earned his Ph.D. in African American Studies from Harvard University, and he holds a B.S. from Oral Roberts University and an M.Div. from Boston University. In support of his research, Josef has received fellowships from the Louisville Institute for the Study of American Religion, The Fund for Theological Education, Harvard's Charles Warren Center for American History and Princeton University's Center for African American Studies. He has published essays and reviews in *Culture and Religion, Callaloo*, the *Journal for the Scientific Study of Religion*, and *PNEUMA: Journal of the Society for Pentecostal Studies*. Josef is currently at work on two book projects: a monograph that analyzes the significance of religion and spirituality in debates regarding racial aesthetics, and an edited volume that explores the sexual politics of black churches.

NOTES

Introduction: The Transformed Nonconformist

[1] Martin Luther King Jr., *Strength to Love* (Philadelphia: Augsburg Fortress, 1981), p. 27.

[2] Anya Kamenetz, *Generation Debt* (New York: Riverhead, 2006), p. 5.

[3] "Turnout by Education, Race and Gender and Other 2008 Youth Voting Statistics" (November 2008), Center for Information and Research on Civic Learning and Engagement (CIRCLE), <www.civicyouth.org/?p=324>.

[4] The 2006 National Civic and Political Health Survey (CPHS) is the most up-to-date and detailed look at how young Americans are participating in politics and communities and their attitudes towards government and current issues. The report examines the civic engagement of young Americans and adults across nineteen core measures of engagement. The report also examines attitudes towards government, levels of political knowledge, partisanship and views of elections and politics. Overall, 1,700 young people ages fifteen to twenty-five were surveyed along with 550 adults ages twenty-six and older between April 27 and June 11, 2006.

[5] "2006 Civic and Political Health of the Nation Survey" (October 2006), Center for Information and Research on Civic Learning and Engagement (CIRCLE), <www.civicyouth.org/research/products/youth_index_2006.htm>.

Chapter 1: Activism Is a Story of Faith

[1] Marshall Ganz, course notes on organizing from "Organizing People, Power, and Change," Harvard Kennedy School of Government, 2006.

[2] Ibid.

[3] Love To Know Encyclopedia Project, s.v. "Hillel" <http://1911encyclopedia.org/Hillel>.

[4] Ganz, course notes.

[5] Ibid.

[6] Ibid.

[7] The exodus narrative has served as a foundational text for liberation theology and freedom movements across the world. God stands on the side of the oppressed, taking an intimate interest in the plight of the Israelites when God says, "I have observed the misery of my people who are in Egypt; I have heard their cry on account of their taskmasters. Indeed, I know their sufferings, and I have come down to deliver them from the Egyptians, and to bring them up out of that land to a good and broad land,

a land flowing with milk and honey" (Exodus 3:7-8 NRSV).

[8]Judge Edwin Cameron, International AIDS Conference, quoted in "Stark Warning over Aids Apathy," *BBC News World Edition,* July 10, 2000 <http://news.bbc.co.uk/2/hi/africa/826979.stm>.

[9]Peter Piot, "Don't Give Up the Fight" (speech at the 17th International AIDS Conference, Mexico City, Mexico, August 3, 2008) <http://data.unaids.org/pub/SpeechEXD/2008/20080803_sp_piot_en.pdf>.

Chapter 2: Getting to the Root Cause of Injustice

[1]Barna Group, "Engaging Churches to Address Global Health and Poverty," February 26, 2009.

[2]Lance Buhl, *Renewing Struggles for Social Justice: A Primer for Transformative Leaders,* CSF Monograph 3 (Durham, N.C.: Duke University, 2008) <http://sanford.duke.edu/centers/clpv/csf/Renewing_2nd_edition.pdf>.

[3]Michael Sandel, *Justice: What's the Right Thing To Do?* (New York: Farrar, Straus & Giroux, 2009), p. 19.

[4]Ibid., p. 20.

[5]Aaron Graham, personal interview, August 2009.

[6]Ibid.

[7]CSF Monograph 4.

[8]Doug Shipman serves as the executive director of the Center for Civil and Human Rights Partnership. Established in February 2007, the partnership was formed in order to undertake predevelopment activities related to the Center for Civil and Human Rights.

[9]Doug Shipman, personal interview, August 2009.

[10]Chris LaTondress, personal interview, August 2009.

[11]Jürgen Moltmann, *On Human Dignity: Political Theology and Ethics* (Philadelphia: Fortress, 1984), p. 22.

[12]Ron Sider, "For the Common Good," *Sojourners* 36, no. 4 (April 2007): 24-29.

[13]Ibid.

[14]Ibid.

[15]Glen Stassen and David Gushee, *Kingdom Ethics: Following Jesus in Contemporary Context* (Downers Grove, Ill.: InterVarsity Press, 2003), p. 20.

[16]Ibid., p. 365.

[17]Obery Hendricks, *The Politics of Jesus* (New York: Doubleday, 2006), pp. 115-23.

[18]"Combating Conflict Diamonds," Global Witness <www.globalwitness.org/pages/en/conflict_diamonds.html>.

[19]Obery Hendricks, *The Politics of Jesus* (New York: Doubleday, 2006), pp. 145-47.

[20]"Injustice Today," International Justice Mission (IJM) <www.ijm.org/ourwork/injusticetoday>.

[21]James Washington, *A Testament of Hope: The Essential Writings of Martin Luther King Jr.* (San Francisco: HarperCollins, 1986), p. 255.

[22]Stassen and Gushee, *Kingdom Ethics*, p. 349.

[23]Ibid., p. 363.

Chapter 3: Following a Holistic Jesus

[1]Obery Hendricks, *The Politics of Jesus: Rediscovering the True Revolutionary Nature*

of Jesus' Teachings and How They Have Been Corrupted (New York: Doubleday, 2006), pp. 5-6.

[2]Howard Thurman, *Jesus and the Disinherited* (Boston: Beacon, 1996), p. 21.

[3]Glen Stassen and David Gushee, *Kingdom Ethics: Following Jesus in Contemporary Context* (Downers Grove, Ill.: InterVarsity Press, 2003), p. 128.

[4]Ibid.

[5]Ibid., p. 132.

[6]Ibid., p. 20.

[7]Ibid., p. 51.

[8]Ibid., p. 132.

[9]Ibid., p. 357.

[10]Jim Wallis, *The Great Awakening: Reviving Faith and Politics in a Post–Religious Right America* (San Francisco: HarperOne, 2006), p. 58.

[11]Ibid.

[12]Brian McLaren, *Everything Must Change* (Nashville: Thomas Nelson, 2007), pp. 2-3.

[13]David Kinnaman and Gabe Lyons, *unChristian* (Grand Rapids: Baker Books, 2007), p. 24.

[14]Ibid., p. 34.

[15]In a chapter of the book *The Justice Project*, ed. Brian D. McLaren, Elisa Padilla and Ashley Bunting Seeber (Grand Rapids: Baker Books, 2009), I identify three common ways that Christians misappropriate Jesus' message and identity.

[16]Jim Wallis, *The Call to Conversion: Why Faith Is Always Personal but Never Private* (New York: HarperSanFrancisco, 2005), pp. 9-10.

[17]"Micah Declaration on Integral Mission (2001)," Micah Challenge <www.micah challenge.us/about/about-us.html>.

[18]Americans in particular have a deeply ingrained aversion and suspicion toward socialism. For some generations this is a remnant of the Cold War struggle between capitalism and communism. For others, it is tied into the uncritical ascension of the free market system.

[19]National Association of Evangelicals, "For the Health of the Nation: An Evangelical Call to Civic Responsibility," 2004, p. 5.

[20]John Howard Yoder, *For the Nations* (Grand Rapids: Eerdmans, 1997), p. 223.

[21]Ibid., p. 235.

[22]Chuck Gutenson, "Constantinianism of the Left?" *Imitatio Christi*, February 26, 2007 <http://imitatiochristi.blogs.com/imitatio_christi/2007/02/constantinianis .html>.

[23]United States Conference of Catholic Bishops, "Faithful Citizenship," 2003, p. 29.

Chapter 4: Pragmatic Solidarity and Hopeful Activism

[1]Paul Farmer, *Pathologies of Power: Health, Human Rights, and the New War on the Poor* (Berkeley: University of California Press, 2003), p. 146.

[2]Ibid., p. 157.

[3]Melinda Miles and Eugenia Charles, *Let Haiti Live: Unjust Policies Toward Its Oldest Neighbor* (Coconut Creek, Fla.: Educa Vision, 2004), p. 31.

[4]Ibid.

[5]Steven Stanek, "Will the World Honour Its Commitments to Haiti?" *The National*, January 22, 2010.

[6]Charles Marsh, *The Beloved Community: How Faith Shapes Social Justice, from the Civil Rights Movement to Today* (New York: Basic Books, 2005), p. 88.

[7]Ibid., p. 107.

[8]Ibid.

[9]Ibid., p. 92.

[10]Ibid.

[11]"Student Nonviolent Coordinating Committee Founding Statement," *The Sixties Project* <www2.iath.virginia.edu/sixties/HTML_docs/Resources/Primary/Mani festos/SNCC_founding.html>

[12]Cleveland Sellers with Robert Terrell, *The River of No Return* (Jackson: University Press of Mississippi, 1990), p. 188.

[13]Marsh, *Beloved Community*, p. 114.

[14]Ibid., p. 118.

[15]Obery Hendricks, *The Politics of Jesus* (New York: Doubleday, 2006), pp. 103-8.

[16]Brian Swarts was the former executive director of the Oregon Center for Christian Values and the Micah Challenge USA, and now works for the Salvation Army.

[17]Jürgen Moltmann, *Theology of Hope* (Philadelphia: Fortress, 1993), p. 10.

[18]Ibid., p. 20.

[19]Howard Thurman, *Jesus and the Disinherited* (Boston: Beacon, 1996), pp. 21, 29.

[20]Samantha Power, "The AIDS Rebel," *The New Yorker*, May 19, 2003, p. 54.

[21]Treatment Action Campaign website, "About the Treatment Action Campaign" <www.tac.org.za/community/about>.

Chapter 5: The Character of Transformed Nonconformism

[1]Dennis Jacobsen, *Doing Justice: Congregations and Community Organizing* (Minneapolis: Fortress Press, 2001), p. 181.

[2]Marshall Ganz, "Organizing: People Power and Change" (class notes from the course of the same name taken at Harvard's Kennedy School of Government in Cambridge, Mass., in 2006).

[3]Kimberely A. Bobo, Jackie Kendall and Steve Max, *Organizing for Social Change: Midwest Academy: Manual for Activists* (Santa Ana, Calif.: Seven Locks Press, 2001), p. 33.

[4]Ibid.

[5]Ganz, "Organizing" notes.

[6]Marshall Ganz, *Why David Sometimes Wins* (New York: Oxford University Press, 2009), p. 10.

[7]Ibid., p. 14.

[8]James Washington, *Testament of Hope: The Essential Writings of Martin Luther King Jr.* (San Francisco: HarperCollins, 1986), p. 255.

[9]"Bali: People Power Confronts Climate Change" <www.avaaz.org/en/bali_report_ back>.

[10]"Burma Report Back: Avaaz Members Donate over $325,000 to the Burmese Democracy Movement" <www.avaaz.org/en/burma_report_back>.

[11]Avaaz.org website <www.avaaz.org/en/about.php>.

[12]Ganz, "Organizing" notes.

[13]Nelson Mandela, quoting Marianne Williamson, *A Return to Love* (New York: HarperCollins, 1992), pp. 190-91.

[14]Marshall Ganz, "Organizing" notes.

[15]Analysis of Federal Election Commission data, Brookings Institution Press, 2008.

[16] Martin Luther King Jr., *Where Do We Go from Here: Chaos or Community?* (Boston: Beacon, 1968), p. 38.

[17]Ganz, "Organizing" notes.

[18]Brian Swarts, personal interview, August 2009.

[19]Advent Conspiracy <www.adventconspiracy.org/>.

[20]Ronald Sider, *The Scandal of the Evangelical Conscience: Why Are Christians Living Just Like the Rest of the World?* (Grand Rapids: Baker Books, 2005), p. 21.

[21]"Cost of Winning a Seat," The Campaign Finance Institute <www.cfinst.org/data/pdf/VitalStats_t1.pdf>.

[22]William Fox, "Address to the People of Great Britain, on the Propriety of Abstaining from West India Sugar and Rum," 1791, quoted in Mimi Sheller, *Consuming the Caribbean* (New York: Routledge, 2003), p. 89.

Chapter 6: Redeeming the American Dream: From Rugged Individualism to the Beloved Community

[1]James Truslow Adams, *Epic of America* (New York: Little, Brown, 1931).

[2]Melvin Oliver and Thomas Shapiro, "Sub-Prime as a Black Catastrophe," *The American Prospect*, September 22, 2008.

[3]Obery Hendricks, *The Politics of Jesus: Rediscovering the True Revolutionary Nature of Jesus' Teachings and How They Have Been Corrupted* (New York: Doubleday, 2006), p. 93.

[4]Lance Buhl, *Renewing Struggles for Social Justice: A Primer for Transformational Leaders*, chap. 7 <http://sanford.duke.edu/centers/clpv/csf/Renewing_2nd_edition.pdf>.

[5]Desmond Tutu, quoted in Trudy Govier, *Forgiveness and Revenge* (New York: Routledge, 2002), p. 97.

[6]Quoted in Charles Marsh, *The Beloved Community: How Faith Shapes Social Justice, from the Civil Rights Movement to Today* (New York: Basic Books, 2005), p. 48.

[7]Marlon Millner, personal interview, August 2009.

[8]Buhl, *Renewing Struggles*, p. 66.

[9]Marsh, *Beloved Community*, pp. 84-86.

[10]Wayne Gordon, "CCDA Philosophy," Christian Community Development Association website <www.ccda.org/philosophy>.

Chapter 7: New Wine for a Changed World

[1]John Perkins, *Let Justice Roll Down* (Grand Rapids: Regal, 1976).

[2]United Nations, The Millennium Development Goals Report 2009.

[3]John Brouwer, *The Year of Jubilee: A Call for Liberation, Distribution, and Restoration*. This study was published in 1979 by the Institute of Christian Studies (Toronto). In 1999 it was republished by Potchefstroomse Universiteit in South Africa.

[4]Chuck Collins, *The Moral Measure of the Economy* (Maryknoll, N.Y.: Orbis, 2007).

[5]See <http://hdr.undp.org/en/statistics/faq/question,68,en.html>.

Chapter 8: Racial Reconciliation and Racial Justice

[1]W. E. B. DuBois, *The Souls of Black Folk* (New York: A. C. McClurg, 1903), p. 13.

[2]Andrew Hacker, *Two Nations: Black and White, Separate, Hostile, Unequal* (New York: Scribner, 2003), p. ix.

[3]Curtiss DeYoung, "All Churches Should Be Multiracial: The Biblical Case," *Christianity Today* 49, no. 4 (April 2005), p. 33 <www.christianitytoday.com/ct/2005/april/22.33.html>.

[4]Ibid.

[5]Roger Simon, "What Happened to Post-Racial America?" *Politico*, August 7, 2009 <www.politico.com/news/stories/0809/25890.html>.

[6]Harry Reid, quoted in John Heilemann and Mark Halperin, *Game Change* (New York: Harper, 2010), p. 37.

[7]Matt Bai, "Is Obama the End of Black Politics?" *The New York Times Magazine*, August 6, 2008, p. 11 <www.nytimes.com/2008/08/10/magazine/10politics-t.html?pagewanted=1&_r=1>.

[8]Stephanie Smith, "Doubling of Maternal Deaths in U.S. 'Scandalous,' Rights Group Says," CNN Health, March 12, 2010 <www.cnn.com/2010/HEALTH/03/12/maternal.mortality/index.html>; Kati Haycock and Eric Hanushek, "An Effective Teacher in Every Classroom," *EducationNext* 10, no. 3 (summer 2010) <http://educationnext.org/an-effective-teacher-in-every-classroom/>; State of Black America, "National Urban League's State Of Black America Report, Released Today, Offers Jobs Plan to Put Urban America Back to Work," March 24, 2010 <www.nul.org/content/state-black-america-jobs>.

[9]Dedrick Muhammad, "40 Years Later: The Unrealized American Dream," April 2008, p. 9 <www.ips-dc.org/files/173/40YearsLater.pdf>.

[10]Emmanuel Lartey, *In Living Color: An Intercultural Approach to Pastoral Care and Counseling* (London: Kingsley, 2003), p. 166.

[11]Ibid., p. 169.

[12]Ibid., p. 166.

[13]Eibach, cited in Leonard Pitts Jr., " 'Post-Racial' America Isn't Here Yet," CNN Politics.com <www.cnn.com/2009/POLITICS/03/28/pitts.black.america/index.html>.

[14]Cornel West, *Race Matters* (New York: Vintage Books, 1994), p. 18.

[15]Barack Obama, "Text of Obama's Fatherhood Speech," Politico, June 15, 2008 <www.politico.com/news/stories/0608/11094.html>.

[16]Chris Rice, "Reconciliation as the Mission of God: Christian Mission in a World of Destructive Conflicts," Duke Divinity School Center for Reconciliation (2005), p. 20 <http://divinity.duke.edu/reconciliation/pdf/reconciliatonasthemissionofgod.pdf>.

[17]Gary Orfield, *Reviving the Goal of an Integrated Society: A 21st Century Challenge* (Los Angeles: The Civil Rights Project/Proyecto Derechos Civiles at UCLA, 2009), <www.civilrightsproject.ucla.edu/research/deseg/reviving_the_goal_mlk_2009.pdf>, p. 3.

[18]Ibid., p. 6.

[19]Ibid., p. 3.

[20]Ibid., p. 4.

[21]Ibid.

[22]The Sentencing Project, "Reducing Racial Disparity in the Criminal Justice System: A Manual for Practitioners and Policymakers," September 2008, p. 2 <www.sentencingproject.org/doc/publications/rd_reducingracialdisparity.pdf>.

[23]Bakari Kitwana, *The Hip Hop Generation* (New York: Basic Civitas, 2002), p. xii.

[24]Suzanne Lipsky, "Internalized Racism," *RC Journal,* 2, 1995 <www.rc.org/publica
tions/journals/black_reemergence/br2/br2_5_sl.html>.

Chapter 9: From Narrow Nationalist to Global Citizen
[1]Richard Land, *The Divided States of America* (Nashville: Thomas Nelson, 2007), p.
37.
[2]Gayle Smith, "In Search of Sustainable Security," Center for American Progress,
June 19, 2008, pp. 2-4.
[3]*U.S. in the World: Talking Global Practice with Americans: A Practical Guide* (New
York: Rockefeller Brothers, 2006).
[4]Samantha Power, *"A Problem from Hell":* America and the Age of Genocide (New
York: Basic Books, 2002), p. xxi.
[5]Save Darfur, "What Has Happened in Darfur," <www.savedarfur.org/pages/
primer>.

Chapter 10: From Solely Service to Civic Discipleship
[1]Aaron Graham, personal interview, August, 2009.
[2]Ibid.
[3]Urbana 09, Advocacy & Poverty Track <www.urbana09.org/tracks.advocacy.cfm>.
[4]Human Wrong Initiative to Stop Child Slavery <www.humanwrong.org/>.
[5]The following is a page from the Human Wrong Campaign, where you can ask members of U.S. Congress to support the Child Protection Compact Act <https://
secure2.convio.net/wv/site/Advocacy?cmd=display&page=UserAction&id=322>.
[6]Chris LaTondresse, personal interview, August, 2009.
[7]Harry Fosdick, *The Meaning of Service* (New York: Abingdom, 1920), p. 18.
[8]Anya Kamenetz, *Generation Debt* (New York: Riverhead, 2006), p. vii.
[9]Ibid., p. 14.
[10]Ibid., p. 5.
[11]Ibid., p. 19.
[12]Onleilove Alston, personal interview, August, 2009.
[13]Tyler Wigg-Stevenson, personal interview, August, 2009.
[14]Reverend Heber Brown III, personal interview, August, 2009. Brown is the pastor of
Pleasant Hill Baptist Church in Baltimore, Maryland.
[15]Leslie Tune, personal interview, August, 2009.
[16]Adam Phillips, personal interview, August, 2009.
[17]Brian Swarts, personal interview, August, 2009.
[18]Aaron Graham, personal interview, August, 2009.
[19]Andrew Wilkes, personal interview, August, 2009.
[20]John James, "Treat-Your-Workers.org; International Coca-Cola Protest October
17," The Body, October 18, 2002 <www.thebody.com/content/art31828.html>

Conclusion: A Lifetime Sojourn
[1]Howard Thurman, "How Good to Center Down," in *Meditations of the Heart* (Boston: Beacon, 1999), pp. 28-29.
[2]Kirk Byron Jones, *Rest in the Storm* (Valley Forge, Penn.: Judson Press, 2001).
[3]Oscar Romero, quoted by Xavier Alpasa on Posterous, October 27, 2009, at <http://
tedfellows.posterous.com/prophets-of-a-future-not-our-own>.

ACKNOWLEDGMENTS

An African proverb, "It takes a village to raise a child," also applies to the process of writing your first book. his book was made possible by a village of supporters, contributors and editors.

First and foremost, I want to thank God for giving me the inspiration and will to finish this project.

My writing was enhanced by the sheer beauty of God's creation, including time that I spent in the Christiania lodge at Vail, a cabin in the mountains of West Virginia, my favorite "thinking" rock in Bellingham, Washington, a picturesque house on Vashon Island, and my wife's and my favorite bed and breakfast: House Mountain Inn in Lexington, Virginia. Specifically I want to thank Paul Johnston, the Harris family, Kay Rich and Rev. Glenn Palmberg for their generous hospitality.

I'm grateful to a number of fellow "transformed nonconformists" whom I had the privilege of interviewing while writing the book and whose stories provide living testimony of what it means to mobilize hope.

Additionally, I want to thank my seminary, Samuel Dewitt Proctor School of Theology, for helping me complete the journey to ordained ministry.

I appreciate the editorial support of Aaron Graham, Duane Shank, Dr. Peter Heltzel, Nick Maynard, Elizabeth Denlinger, my parents Christopher and Saundra Taylor, and last but certainly not least, the creative genius of my editor Dave Zimmerman at IVP.

I need to thank my beloved wife, Sharee, who exhibited resilient patience and offered constant encouragement—even as the book took on a life of its own, displacing many of our date nights and causing its fair share of stress.

Finally, I want to dedicate this book to my son. I pray that he grows up in a world transformed by a cadre of creative, maladjusted people mobilizing hope for generations to come.

Rev. Adam Taylor

LIKEWISE. *Go and do.*

....

A man comes across an ancient enemy, beaten and left for dead. He lifts the wounded man onto the back of a donkey and takes him to an inn to tend to the man's recovery. Jesus tells this story and instructs those who are listening to "go and do likewise."

Likewise books explore a compassionate, active faith lived out in real time. When we're skeptical about the status quo, Likewise books challenge us to create culture responsibly. When we're confused about who we are and what we're supposed to be doing, Likewise books help us listen for God's voice. When we're discouraged by the troubled world we've inherited, Likewise books encourage us to hold onto hope.

In this life we will face challenges that demand our response. Likewise books face those challenges with us so we can act on faith.

....

likewisebooks.com

....